LEADERSHIP CULTURE

WHAT MAKES OR BREAKS A LEADER?

MALA THAPAR

First published in 2022 by Hansib Publications
76 High Street, Hertford, SG14 3TA, UK

info@hansibpublications.com
www.hansibpublications.com

Copyright © Mala Thapar, 2022
malavthapar@hotmail.com

ISBN 978-1-912662-58-6
ISBN 978-1-912662-59-3 (Kindle)
ISBN 978-1-912662-60-9 (ePub)

Mala Thapar has asserted her moral right to be identified as the author of this work.

All rights reserved. No part of this publication may be reproduced, stored in a retrieval system, or transmitted, in any form or by any means, electronic, mechanical, photocopying, recording or otherwise, without the prior permission of the author.

Printed in Great Britain

*Dedicated to
Her Majesty Queen Elizabeth II, for her
exemplary leadership,
and to the leader in each of us in every walk
of life who has potential but is afraid of
facing this truth because the neuro- patterns
in his brain make the decisions for him.*

*To the students of JOA
Enjoy the read.
Male
11.3.22*

INTRODUCTION

I remember an Indian politician who went to collect votes door to door. When asked "What would he do for the people if elected the third time?" He smiled and said: "First time, I looked after my needs, next time of those around me, it is your turn now." He won the election on grounds of 'honesty'. People trusted his candour hoping it was their turn to be served now.

This book explores leadership from two stands: Positional and Relational in a social and cultural context. It emphasizes building trust and candour – two pillars on which the Head rests. Both are complimentary not contradictory. While one form focuses on the positioning, the other builds on relationships. Trust is the cement that binds and is built brick by brick. There is no commanding it, but there is breaking it by insensitivity and inconsistency in words and actions. To some degree, leadership is relational selling of agendas, tasks, building teams and doing network marketing. It is data collection and filing. But more than that it is a network of relationships.

I ask the question: *"Does the position determine the conduct of the leader, or does the leader determine positioning the seat?"* Tricky question with variables. Yet, one question should be asked when interviewing for the position of a leader. *"Why do you choose this post?"* The answers often get embezzled in being theoretically correct but practically incompetent. Hence, the experiential aspect of leadership is foremost in the selection process. *How broad based is it, what are the values, perceptions, perspectives on which the person not the seat operates. Are these aligned with the corporate or educational values? What strategies, processes and problem solving techniques are involved?*

I remember a person entering a hall for being interviewed. He faced a board of interviewees. There was a chair in his way, and he was carrying a lot of files and folders. He tripped and fell. Getting up, he looked at the board and said, "At least I fell in the right company." This won him the post.

Presence of mind worked. Welcome aboard to the flight of Leadership – unfasten perceptions.

The use of the masculine pronoun throughout the text is purely for the sake of convenient grammatical expression. It is not meant to present a male-centred or male-oriented approach to the analysis. MT

CONTENTS

INTRODUCTION 5

Chapter One
NUTS AND BOLTS OF LEADERSHIP 8

Chapter Two
LEADERSHIP ANALYSED 15

Chapter Three
DIFFERENT KINDS OF LEADERSHIP 40

Chapter Four
POSITIONAL LEADERSHIP 45

Chapter Five
RELATIONAL LEADERSHIP 61

Chapter Six
POSITIONAL AND RELATIONAL LEADERSHIP 84

Chapter Seven
EFFECTIVE LEADERSHIP 88

Chapter Eight
CANDOUR 95

Chapter Nine
CONCLUSION 98

ACKNOWLEDGEMENTS 103

BIBLIOGRAPHY 105

CHAPTER ONE

NUTS AND BOLTS OF LEADERSHIP

Some believe leaders are born, not made. Others feel leadership is taught in schools. I feel it to be a combination of the two. Take the example of Lincoln and Gandhi. Both had the characteristics of a leader having gone through the fires and felt the heat. They had the courage to speak up against falsehood and like Christ be ready to take the brunt of being themselves and standing up for principles. In their consistency lay seeds of power. In their humility their charm and results. Not one fought violently. They did not have to put another down. They had to accentuate the positive. This is what leaders do. They accentuate the positive. They do not judge to discriminate, slam doors, or diminish another. Raw materials like sound habits must be present to be built upon and augmented by education and experience. Leadership is a part and parcel of one's mindset. Minds are set at different frequencies depending upon our perception, patterns of behaviour, upbringing and experience. All these educate us. When we go in for a degree, it is our information that gets acknowledged not our education.

This writing aims at exploring the nuts and bolts of leadership. It addresses future leaders with questions and reflections, anecdotes, and introspection. Those who are not identified as leaders but darn the role of a leader, regularly play the role. I remember a man walking in the park with his five year old son. The boy was temperamental and kept stamping the ground asking for his way and troubling the man. The man kept saying, "Well done Tom, keep going." When I heard him say this a couple of times, my curiosity was raised. I could not help but ask: "But Tom is bothering you, why are you saying well done, Tom?" The man looked at me briefly and said: "It is I who am Tom; he is my son Jerry. I am commending my patience with him."

What a good way to keep going in life. He was addressing what he could control. Some leaders try to control another before they even think of commanding and controlling their own behaviour of treating others like commodities. What we need to endure becomes easier with a positive stroke. Yet, few leaders use 'humour' to get through situations and avoid new ones. It is a simple but effective way to cross paths.

The young, the old and the in-between are all stepping on the ladder of leadership or followership each day. They tread the globe thumping heavily or tread gently. This depends upon what type of leaders they envisage themselves to be, what they want to be remembered for, what legacy they wish to leave behind. And what attributes they bring to the table. How they handle themselves determines their and the organization's success or failure. It defines their maturity and character. I remember my mother's words: "Wealth lost, nothing lost, health lost something lost, character lost, everything lost." Leadership needs character more than hegemony.

The trajectory of leadership requires careful studying of the flora and fauna before landscaping a change. Coming in heavy with expectations and an agenda is a self defeating exercise. This writing is the outcome of leadership training during my growing years. My parents entrusting me with the responsibility of my grandparents and younger sister gave me a head start into planning, executing, managing, prioritizing activities to meet the needs of all concerned. This was followed by leadership roles as the head girl of the school, president of the college, Director of Research and Development, and being the wife of the commanding officer. Fr S.J. Wirth who held leadership training sessions and trained me to introduce these in Loreto convent. Each role had its expectations. I learnt along the way, by making mistakes. The one lesson I honed early in life was of **listening with humility** and **expressing with clarity**. I was wary of giving the custody of my mind to another. I walked into situations with **honesty, resolve** and **integrity**. I learnt from these three masters. Being my authentic self and voicing my feelings has been important to me since I was born, and this has had its upside and downside. I have lost friends who took my trust but not my candour. Candour is the outcome of trust.

Results do not make or break a leader. But being unfaithful to oneself does break one slowly, like acid it eats into the skin to find how empty and dissipated the layers are. One has to live with oneself twenty four seven and others some of the time. My mentors took time and effort to communicate, give me a feedback and be my mirror, validating and correcting.

I invite you to explore two kinds of leadership: **Positional and Relational**. Both stand on the ability to respond i.e., response-ability. It is my endeavour to look into both these realms. What shapes the person behind the seat and how he affects others. History is replete with examples of leaders who became the positions they held, and those who influenced the position they held. Both served. The question is: *Who did they serve? What did they achieve and for who?* The answer to these questions makes or mars leadership.

Unfortunately, most power mongers get into these positions after promising themselves and the public their intent to serve.

The seesaw of leadership is seen through the lens of values, vision and follow ups. Like two sides of the coin, two aspects of relationship positional and relational are inter-related. Yet, they stand independent of each other when they do not communicate. Similar to marriages where partners who live together but do not communicate. There are no clear demarcation lines. The see-saw approach is bi-polar and subject to the leader's mood swings, his appetites and his integrity or lack of it. People promise much then back off from their promises, leaving those who trusted their word in a lurch. Whatever their personal reasons, they forget the moral imperative of their decisions and the ripple effect it will have on others.

Positional leadership builds walls and relational leadership builds bridges. While positional leadership affects those under its realm considerably and often negatively; relational leadership is democratic in nature and allows for growth.

The question is "Does the person occupying the chair make it or does the chair make the person? People have varied perceptions, perspectives and priorities. They may come to power with expectations not only for the people they serve but for themselves, ambitions and more. This becomes apparent when their character asserts itself in small and big decisions, execution, policies, assessments, and judgements.

Bosses are not always leaders and vice versa. Who is an effective leader and what does it take to be one? These questions are explored in depth. There is no cookie cutter strategy to make leaders. Courses and degrees may inform but they do not create leaders. Experiences do. Leaders are good readers of practical and theoretical demands. They are conscious and caring.

The bottom line is *"Are leaders readers of people?"* Because people are readers of leaders. In the act of observing and perceiving, the ladder is climbed, retained, made fruitful or descended. This elucidates the principles of leadership. It deals with day-to-day crisis. Also with last minute decision making, with exercises that strengthen the muscles of the mind and the heart. It explores the questions:

"How much of leadership is learnt in the classroom of life? Do people follow you because they want to or because they have to? Are you the position calling the shots, or the person encouraging others to call them? What is leadership, the 'chair', or the 'persona'?

The greatest worry is when leaders address expectations, based on their assumptions. They fumble and fall. In their excitement and enthusiasm, they do not reflect, listen to the unsaid the unheard, the undone. Seeing patterns and observing body language goes a long way in comprehending the landscape. The skill set needed for a leader is far greater than what is mentioned or expected from the position. It involves 'being human'. No child ever learnt to walk without falling down. No horse trainer has gone without being kicked. Leadership is training ground. The position is where one is posited. The ground is mushy as there are differences, baggage, expectations, and one's own fallacies and incompetence. To manage all this and come out unscathed is Herculean.

Yet, this is expected of leaders. Leadership is 'not a popularity contest'. Nor is it a dictation of terms and conditions. It is a 'portfolio' like any other. To understand it, we need to study it. Then comprehend it. Reflect before executing it. The greatest enemy of leadership is **assumptive** behaviours stemming out of **parochial perceptions.** These become walls in communication.

Simple overt communication is the key to avoiding situations. **Kindness** over manipulations; **Comradery** over silos; **Service** before self three important lessons, I learnt on the road. It also involves having resilience as there are bound to be pitfalls, unpopularity, and stress. Preparing for these helps. Embracing uncertainty is power over circumstance.

Often leaders skip preparation in the rush to reach targets and meet ends; or they delegate it to a junior. While delegation is division of task and convenient for the leader, it is not the answer to being thorough. It keeps the leader from thinking, reflecting and assessing before delivering his lines. He speaks out of another's mind not his own. This takes away authenticity and loses impact. Impromptu speech scores over a prepared one, when a leader is just reading off another's words.

Connecting, resolving, negotiating and most importantly empathy and emotional intelligence are a long list of requirements that come with making mistakes. Welcome to the journey of the making of a leader.

CHAPTER TWO

LEADERSHIP ANALYSED

Leadership is a love story with its labour lost in perceptions. Yet, most crave for the position. It makes them somebody, gives them temporal power over others. Little do they realize the price of power is at conflict with the price of conscience. Sooner or later, this becomes a battleground. We seek what we cannot fully achieve, as interdependence and collective consciousness are at play. This puzzle can be solved by intrapersonal and interpersonal relationships. Therefore, leadership is all about relationship forming, maintaining, and tending to. Time is the key ingredient as it never returns. We think we can attend to relationships later, but no. They whiz from one's attention and are gone. People unlike objects cannot be twisted around. WE all have been on the other side of the pavilion playing the game.

Leaders wear many hats, play many roles, but in each of these the following come in handy: Listening, Reflecting and Introspection. Optimism is an expectation from the leader. No one wants to be led by a pessimist. Right associations and non assumptive behaviours prevent difficult situations. Integrity and consistency are two pillars and crutches. These make for character and the persona. We get so caught up with the personality of the leader, that we lose track of Substance, Values, Integrity, and Vision.

Packaging is not everything. Subscribing to the Celebrity Culture reminds us that "They would not be wolves if we were not sheep."[1] This writing examines Expectations, Challenges, and Key Ingredients in the recipe of Leadership. It takes the specific and sees it universally applicable.

The word leadership has ten alphabets nee templates. Each one stands for a trait that assists in the composition of a leader. When leadership is defined alphabetically it reads as:

- **L** Listening and love.
- **E** Empathy is the fellow feeling we all need and crave. It connects and creates harmony.
- **A** Attitude is a small thing that makes a huge difference in building momentum and rapport.
- **D** Dexterity, discernment, and diversity. Dexterity is the ability to deal with diversity with a spirit of accommodation and skill. It is wearing multiple hats as the time requires and rising to the plate. Discernment is key to distinguishing the talent, the nature of the job and assigning accordingly. And diversity needs an attitude of inclusion.
- **E** Evolving and energizing with role modelling.
- **R** Respect, Resilience and Reciprocation: These three attributes mark the cornerstones of each turn in the journey.

---

1. Shakespeare in *Julius Caeser*

S Synchronization here applies to doing many things at the same time with co-ordination and cooperation. IT adds meaning and speeds the task in hand. It builds teams by shared vision and values.

H Honouring those who honour us regardless of anyone's perceptions, circumstance or where they are posited.

I Initiating change, being innovative in problem solving, addressing issues and bringing creativity to the field.

P Principles are the bedrock and they rest on flexibility. They are not fixations nor unmoving glaciers, there are exceptions to every rule, and it is here that discernment kicks in.

LISTENING: Listening is learning. It is of two types: **Active and Passive**. Most leaders love to give talks to gain attention, to make their viewpoint and agenda known. Seldom do they read the air, as Japanese say. Rarely do they sense the mood of the crowd, the other and the need of the hour. It is as if a tape is playing through their heads, and they must push their agenda. People have no choice but to lap it up. They have no chance at conversations. These are so few, and in between. Knowing when to speak and when to shut up, is very succinctly put in a book by Dr. Michael D. Sedler called *When to Speak up and when to Shut up*. In this book he explores the cost and purpose of silence. He emphasizes not to hold down feelings, not to shut down and keep ideas inside. He proposes direct personal contact and not using a go between. It always complicates matters creating situations hard to get out of. Church leaders become isolated and insulated by the laws they make, the behaviours they keep, the image they protect. Meetings consist of leaders talking and others taking notes. Few listen. Listening lets them know what they do not know. There is always something even if a perspective that we have blinded ourselves to and can be informed about. When this is ignored, trouble begins.

"Talking only repeats what they already know and are reinstating to those who are supposed to comply and follow them." (H.H. Dalai Lama) It does not bring forward different perspectives, dissent, and knowledge. Hence, assumptions are parochial. Not responding is seen as being arrogant. Reacting negatively is seen as rage and autocracy. Values get diminished when we relate leadership to what is base in us or other people's impressions. WE try to fulfil expectations then and lose the rudder and the radar. God has given us two ears and one mouth so we may listen twice as much as we speak. Listening positively is different from listening negatively and brushing off another. Positive listening is active listening and making a note of what is said, why, where, and how can things be improved to create a win/win situation. Reflecting before responding, seeking clarification, and rendering apology if needed. Those who listen positively last their roles. Those who do not are beguiled by what is in store for them. Soon people get to see and separate the rhetoric from reality. Like a pack of cards their persona falls. What they thought to be strength becomes their weakness. It boils down to perception and whose perception?

EXERCISES: *Have you stood silent when someone was making a bad decision, not acting in the interest of both parties? How did your silence impact the situation? That someone could be your alter self. What did it feel like? Was it a proactive or reactive decision? What excuses do we normally use to stay silent? Are these real or a coping strategy?*

LOVE: Like Love, Leadership is a verb. To be in love with one's work, to love to learn, to love to communicate, these are some of the dimensions of love. With love everything becomes zestful. Something to look forward to. Something new to learn. Something to give and something to take. This two way interaction energizes, calibrates energy, and motivates. It is not a position alone. It is responsibility. One does not fall in love but rises like a cake, or a loaf of bread with yeast and baking powder. The yeast here is the willingness to perceive rightly keeping the other in mind. If one wants to be honoured one must honour. Love is chemistry. It arises from the leader's personality and character. It is spontaneous and can be cultivated too. Intent matters. More than that commitment matters. Courage is key to executing the policy democratically. Sometimes one gets kicked and at other times one has to swallow one's pride. Every horse trainer gets kicked, gets a kick out of it and finally there is a kick start. Similarly taking rebuttals personally creates dis harmony. There is many a slip between the cup and the lip. Not everything said is customized nor should it be. Things get out of hand by connecting the issue to one's personality.

Sensitivity helps but when exceeds its mark it becomes a phobia. Many carry phantoms in their minds. These impressions become projections of behaviour in their dealings with others. They are left with few if any mirrors, because of their sensitivity. They do not encourage candour. With forthright and upfront talk everything under the sun can be cleared. But individuals, nations, bosses seldom approach the issue with an inside out approach. Mostly it is a reaction, a response, a monosyllable, based on their personal bias. When taking a rebuttal, it is best not to be thrown off, to put perspective and maintain our balance.

The leader imbues meaning in the words he chooses. Language conveys more than the message. It conveys a personality, feeling, race, status quo, openness, mindset, prejudice, objective and more. Yet, few choose their words. Most rant them. Anything does not go. Outbursts are serious deficits in a leader's character. They are the rage coming from grief, disappointment, unmet expectations. This is not taught in business schools. Achieving targets is taught but achieving humane results is not. Business ethics is taught but business decorum is not.

Love and the joy derived from one's work, is an example followed. This creates a field of energy and when heightened an aura that attracts, a vibration that calibrates and a character that abides circumstance. It is getting out of the comfort zone to touch the hem of uncomfortable issues, the responsibilities one would not take, and so on, that makes or breaks a leader's reputation. What is left is the puny self in the shadows of what seems like a leadership of convenience. "Uneasy lies the head that wears a crown" (Shakespeare) But it need not.

One does not get to be a leader without first assessing what is expected of him and what he expects in return. It involves introspection and discernment.

What do love and leadership have in common?

EMPATHY: This is 'a' fellow feeling. It is not sympathy. There is equity in empathy. Getting in the shoes of another and feeling what she is feeling, seeing her perspective from her standpoint is what empathy is. It drives home understanding of another's situation, her values and context like nothing else. In doing so it opens a plethora of opportunity to work with the other person, uplift her spirits and build community. This is humanity.

Why then do we cringe and crawl when asked to step up? Is it because of apprehensions born of perceptions and patterns?

EXERCISE: It helps to have one trusted and trusting person or an intimate circle of friends who keep one grounded by acting as a mirror. They are not sycophants but make the leader better. The leader accepts them as they are, not as he wants them to be.

Here is what some great leaders of the past have asked of their close friends:

1. To love them unconditionally
2. To watch the leader's back
3. To be honest with the leader
4. To complement his weaknesses

5. To tell him what he needs to hear not what he wants to hear.
6. To add value to him
7. And to enjoy the journey with him.
8. In return the leader gives loyalty, rewards them financially and with opportunities for growth. Having a strong set of one or two friends or an inner circle prevents loneliness, makes the journey enjoyable, creates a family atmosphere and prevents hubris.

ATTITUDE is cultivated and has immense range. It makes or breaks a leader. "Attitude not Aptitude is seen to have determined Altitude." My observations and lived experiences prove the point. Attitude is the mail that waits to be answered and the mail that is promptly answered. It all depends upon attitude, how we wish to attend to the matter, what position we take in leadership: relational or positional. Attitude is not what one is born with. One imbibes it. It is conditioned, copied, and enforced by the people around us. It arises from their patterns patterning on our psyche. Their actions and reactions form us. Therefore, education of the heart and the mind are equally important and role models are in great demand.

Attitude in a leader is the ability to stay positive, amidst negative circumstances, be humble, show tenacity and resilience. It boils down to role modelling of what the leader expects from his team. These behaviours are not easy to come by, as the leader is human too. There are expectations on both sides. Hence, mindfulness by deep breathing, taking short breaks during the day helps. Just smiling at everyone cheers and mitigates mistrust and anxieties.

PITFALLS: Some leaders spend their time and energy on wrong people. They develop those who are there for development sake. Those with X factor or those who are winners by nature get left behind because they are not recognized. They may not be forthcoming, be bold and outspoken or may incur the displeasure of the leader by not meeting his expectations.

It is best to start in a neutral way and not let expectations get in the way. Troublemakers, strugglers, and complainers take up most of the time of a leader. Little time is left to pull out the positive and develop them. When a leader does this, he develops an attitude that not only takes him up but takes the entire team to a place of growth, productivity, and happiness.

DARE AND DEXTERITY: *I was mute with silence. I held my peace even from good; and my sorrow was stirred up.* (Psalm 39:2)

'Dare' here stands for taking calculated risks. It also refers to the ability to stand up to speak, and sit down to listen. It is the language of humility and humanity. Dare to take initiative, be proactive, not follow herd thinking, be original, have and achieve the vision as a team. Dare to sacrifice for the sake of the vision. If you want to accomplish great feats, you need to take calculated risks. People are reluctant to leave their comfort zones. They will fail you; they will implode. They will fight you to your face or behind it. This will force the leader to make a choice between shrinking the vision or stretching people to reach it. The latter makes for effective leadership.

Risk changes relationships. Either people gain confidence by it or if the leader fails, they lose their confidence in him. Relational credibility is at stake; hence people seldom take the risk to get out of their comfort zone unless forced to do so. Sitting by the shore gets you nowhere. Going deep helps procure the pearls. Risk is always present in leadership. Anytime one moves forward on any initiative there will be those who agree and those who do not. Even if you are right the risk does not diminish. This is because there are many perspectives backing many different behaviours. Being the face, the head and heart of his people the leader can make a difference to his organization, his people and in doing so to himself.

ENTHUSIASM: The word enthusiasm is derived from the Greek. To enthuse means to fill with God. It is that breath of spontaneity that welcomes endeavour, potential and effort by appreciation and acknowledgement. It is also the motivation behind all endeavours. Imagine a leader without enthusiasm. It is like a soda without fizz. When we let it stay boxed, we contaminate it with misperceptions. For enthusiasm is life of the living, gift of the giving. It is renewal of the Spirit by sharing enrichment. Its positive vibrations infect another and bring about encouragement, passion in work and relationships. Enthusiasm is also mindfulness and focus. It is giving of one's inert and true self to any endeavour or relationship. Evolution of leadership does not merely rest on the leader's shoulders. It is a combination of facts. The fantasy world of tinsel disappears when the leader is faced with real life situations. Like wounds festering unattended he is served these on a plate. What does he do?

Words of Winston Churchill come to mind: *"A pessimist sees difficulty in every opportunity and an optimist sees opportunity in every difficulty."* A sharp leader learns from his people, like a good teacher learns from her students. They are in a relationship. This is not hierarchical but democratic. One's success depends upon mutual endeavour, and this must be clearly understood before arriving at any leadership role. This includes those of parents and others we encounter on life's path. Have the courage and the courtesy to acknowledge, validate, and appreciate another. It builds a fortress of strength. And we all need this to strengthen life's many paths in many ways. A leader helps us to build this. He is a proponent of good values, lasting values, of a broad vision, an open mind that takes criticism gratefully as it does praise. Learn from everybody and every situation. Their evolution depends upon their mindset. The muscles of the mind are numerous and need to be identified. Mind training comes into being. It is not about coaching as much as introspecting and seeing yourself from an unbiased point of view.

Hear other people and invite their feedback. Be candid. Keep personal hurt aside. Take things objectively. Seeing them unbiased by individual perceptions brings truth to the fore. This fosters understanding, Empathy not apathy. Shared perspective. Decisions cast in stone, prevent evolution, and trouble the Spirit. Life and death are a livid example of this.

When we decide for the 'Spirit' we err, for it is the mystery that enthuses and endures. Recognize it and accept it. And see the difference in those you lead or those who lead you.

Evolution of leadership involves risk taking. Discussion before decision. Acquiescence before implementation, are key to avoid singular and assumptive decisions. These impede evolution and dampen enthusiasm. Failure like success is a portal. It need not be permanent. It is a step to opening another venue for growth. Hence, it is to be celebrated and discussed. Closed minds are closed doors. Open minds open doors and communication.

RESPECT: We all know that respect is earned not handed on a platter to a chair. Respect comes from showing responsibility, one's response and more. It cannot be demanded. It is not ongoing nor natural and lasting. To earn respect, one must walk the talk. Respect is not lip service nor is it saying things politely alone. It is substance and form. With dichotomy in substance and delivery the message is lost in oblivion. It frustrates the sender and the receiver. Respect needs to be nurtured day by day, brick by brick, instance by instance. Respect and ego are arch enemies. It is not about winning the race but participating in the race. Heroes emerge from the ordinary humdrum. They are not always strong in body, sharp in mind or more. What stands them apart is their sense of respecting values, vision, humanity, and humility. Their vulnerability becomes their strength. Maintaining integrity takes actions not words. It is Spirit in action. When we worry about how we are perceived we falter, and our expectations shape the results. Let go.

Consistency of character and keeping one's word builds respect and people know they can depend upon you. Consistency is key to maintaining and earning respect. When you sacrifice transparency, you lose respect. When you withhold, you make the other person wonder what is the truth and if you will not change your mind tomorrow. This builds walls. Thoughtfulness and consideration are attributes of high context cultures. People in position read the air, as Japanese would say. They sense before they venture into assessments. Some leaderships dwindle into minuscule management.

STRENGTH: Smart leaders map out their strengths and those of their employees. They begin to maximize on them, demarcate accordingly, plan and execute in keeping in mind strengths and weaknesses. A leader is not just a manager. He is not an executive alone. Leadership is a combination of the two and more. In this more lies the secret. Self awareness is a leadership strength. Situational awareness is another excellent communication and negotiation skill that makes up the plate. *"People ask the difference between a leader and a boss. The leader leads, the boss drives."* (Theodore Roosevelt) Gratitude is a strength, Kindness is a strength, Vulnerability is a strength as it makes a leader more humane, a risk taker and a mistake maker. Owing up is essential and a mark of strength.

HUMOUR: There is a saying: "Life is easy, humour is hard." Humour provides perspective, helps develop clear insights and is a great way of handling a crisis. It becomes a problem-solving strategy that helps one get through the day, a life, and difficult situations. Yet, we forget this and carrying the world on our shoulders the Atlas shrugs passing the buck, blaming another, or puts his hands up, leaving the crew to do as they like, give up or stay with a loss of morale. Humour is uplifting. It builds positive teams, adds proportion, and makes the meal delectable.

Humour is enabling as it lubricates the rough edges of personalities at war with themselves and others. Lincoln was a great storyteller and used funny anecdotes to bring his people around. His personal life was replete with struggles and sorrow, yet he kept his chin up and aided others in doing so. It is another way of diverting from the uncomfortable to the comfortable by bringing levity to the situation. People like that.

Leaders who can laugh at their own folly, show their human side, become easier to deal with and earn trust of others. They show themselves as one of the many, not separate from them, nor over and above them.

INTEGRITY is consistency in dealing with people and oneself. It is keeping one's word. It is cultivated in life's classrooms over decades. Leadership starts with small things and makes its way into larger ones. It is innovation, positive participation, and initiative. Without these leaders they become dummies. Their weakness is sooner or later exposed, for strength does not lie in sinews but in being vulnerable and humble. It lies in being human. Making mistakes and correcting them. It is not a frigid silence but a responsible response. In the crucibles that try our mettle we are one. *Why not in the roles we play? Why does hierarchy rule its play here blindfolding us to this reality?*

PEACE, POSSIBILITY AND PROBABILITY are to leaders what roots are to a tree. These are the foundational rocks on which the edifice of leadership stands. The question asked is, "What is the purpose, the reason, the motivation, or manipulation techniques employed by the leader to reach results of his liking?" What are we as leaders propelling for and pushing against? This defines our role, our goal and us. This determines us as leaders or bosses, it is temporary or lasting. The rider and his horse must be aligned and beat the same rhythm for a smooth ride.

I hope to take sight off the external alone and delve deep into the internal forces that make, break, and sustain a leader. Values that comprise the role are:

1. Introspection and Self-Development
2. Relatability and Accountability
3. Commitment and Consistency
4. Flexibility and Sensitivity
5. Honouring Humility
6. Being Human and Owning mistakes
7. Empathy and Energy
8. Affinity and Adjustability
9. Innovation and Cooperation
10. Initiative and Courage

Introspection and Self-Development: A leader who is a torch to others introspects. He sends time reflecting upon his decisions and is not stubbornly stuck in them. This distinguishes an n effective leader from an egoistic one. Reflections and examining one's conscience build shared perceptions, create creative solutions, and identify people's uniqueness and strength. Ralph Waldo Emerson says that he never met a person who was not his superior in some way. This is a lesson in humility.

Success is not out there. It is here. It emanates from soul searching, being one's authentic self and allowing and accepting others to be the same. Cast in a shell we sometimes forget this and operate from a positional place. When consciousness dawns, harm has been done. Therefore, leaders are good readers of themselves and their people.

Introspection is not making excuses for oneself, nor justifying one's actions and rationalizing them. A leader has to rise above defending himself and begin facing himself. Introspection is looking at and minding one's p's and q's. It raises one from a base level of being to becoming. It helps the visionary process and looks at the leader's values nonjudgmentally. Introspection helps self correction, helps the leader organize his life, time and relationships so as not to be used by it but use it effectively, knowing there is a moral imperative to every decision he makes. When this decision is based upon good judgement coming from introspection, it is flexible and adhering to people.

Relatability: If one cannot relate to a leader, he becomes a phantom in the minds of those he leads. They fear him. At one level the leader may want that unconsciously, but pragmatically this does not foster followership nor is effective. It has a shelf life and withers soon after.

Relatability is not a concept. It is an active verb upon which the foundation of a relationship is built. It is a character trait.

Leaders with deep and sound characters build on relating to others, even after they cease to hold positions. They embody relatability. It is not a functional piece they wear and then take off. It is not transactional but transformative. It energizes the team as well as the leader.

Being able to see things from another's perspective, being inclusive, grateful. Empathic, consistent, co-operative, creative, and caring are all embodied and needed by relatability. These cannot be emphasized enough as it preludes success. It is the very ingredient on which success depends and is built. Take away anyone of these traits and the see-saw of leadership wans. People become wistful and uncertainty bugs both the leader and the follower.

Relatability comes from the willingness to connect, communicate, and relate in matters small and big. It goes beyond a hello. How are you? Or a polite pushing of one's agenda. It does not manipulate the other. It does not build an alibi to make the leader look good and innocent. It faces truth and stands by it. The leader is aware of his inner truth before he can face the outside truth, as both are interconnected.

Commitment and Consistency: Commitment is interpreted in various ways. It is not merely being committed to one's position, but committed to one's character, responsibilities, people, goals and roles and more. Commitment is not a matter of convenience nor is it a one-time thing. It comes with dexterity, is a cultivated art and built daily, renewed like a promise with action steps. *What does commitment look like?*

Arched perspectives and inflexibility leaves people in a limbo, not knowing what comes next. Leader's mood swings bring pitfalls in the organization. Many wonder about their future. So does the leader who exercises power without commitment. He can be committed to his gals and role but not to the people. He can be a persona of multiple personalities but not a character that one can count on. When the negatives are seen and consistently portrayed from apposition of power as shadows lurking in the dark zones of unpredictability, the leader loses big time.

Consistency builds trust and commitment. Without these the leader fumbles and weakens his stance. Yet, these are built over a period of time beginning from early years. If a person bereft of them, he should not get into leadership roles for they are not at the free will for him to darn and dispose. They are acquired by a lifetime of awareness, constant practice, education, environment, and life experiences. This is why a degree or an interview can rarely determine the suitability of a candidate to a leadership position.

What does a committed leader look like and act like? A. He sticks it out through thick and thin. He is not easily perturbed. Taking comments and issues personally and judgmentally makes for weak leadership. Seeing them objectively and staying committed to both the task and the people consistently builds character. It takes gumption. It takes courage. Yet, it is worth it and helps one pull through the difficult times.

Flexibility and Sensitivity: Inflexible decisions make for positional leadership. The latter receive people's least not their best. They are weak, they give their least. Strength lies in what the leader can give, not receive. People don't come to us. They are sent to us. When we shut our mind's doors, we block consciousness. Our choices and decisions are often based on peripheral perceptions. They do not consider the unknown future. Only the intermittent past and the still uncertain and in the making present. Let us not look forward in apprehension nor back with regret. We are more than the past. We are yet to become the enlightened future. Present is for us to reflect, to connect and create the future we want.

Upon reflection on persona, personality, and character, we discover, uncover, and recover. Think about it. It all comes together after the downpour. The road ahead shortens for us all. Question is how do we approach it and what tools are in our kit? The answer is sensitivity and empathy make up care.

Honouring Humility: Humility is an attitude not a mask to wear on and off occasionally. It is built in the character and not something to be strived for. This is the difference between lip service and real service. Humility sits on every table. It knows that it does not know enough. While attitude meets gratitude with entitlement mentality and humility waits for the consequences. Rage is felt but not addressed with rage. Age is considered a repertoire of wisdom. Humility is not age bound, sex bound, position bound. It is liberty itself. That breath of fresh air that will whisk everything to functionality, peace and possibility and probability. Yet, it's not on the business school manual, nor education or leadership program manuals. It sits in the chronicles of scriptures and is spoken about on Sundays.

Humility is the key to prosperity of the fortunate few who live by Grace. When we honour humility, we begin to gain perspective on things. We posit ourselves in a place of empathy. All of us can be edgy. Just as we expect another to understand and withstand the edginess in us, we must honour their edginess by not taking it personally. Many misunderstandings blow away with genuine friends. Those that do not cause anxiety and dis- ease. This distinguishes them from pumped up egos who waffle at the slightest remark that is not in line with their comfort zone, their pleasantries and are afraid to look into their truth with eyes wide open. Honouring humility is honouring another. Living with differences, not shutting them out. Honouring those who honour you. A leader who does not brush away a subordinate or another because of his time constraints and his positional power, reaps long term results and not short term fixes. People are sensitive. They have dignity. They have class. Just because they happen to work for him does not make them any less. It makes them more. This the leader either realizes and shows in his behaviour or does not to his and their peril.

Being Human: Despots have been leaders of a different nature. They think, and act differently. Mind you, they can be charmers, friends who poke you in the back or turn their backs on you. They can achieve much by one standard, 'Theirs'. One missing tool in their armoury is Humanity. *Is it because they want quick results, are impatient, insecure, cling to power, so do not think of another with empathy?*

Forgiveness unasked liberates. To err is human to forgive divine. Being human may not reach you to heights of temporal power. It may not put you in the limelight nor keep the limelight on you. But it certainly lights a lamp within you. The light of this spreads. It illuminates dark corners and heals many an aching heart.

What does being human look like? It is that look of understanding. That kind word another so wants to hear. Being there for another when they need us most. Hearing another's story without value judgement attached to it. It is those little everyday nibbling that make or break the fabric of society. Discerning them, reaching out and reaching within to look at our reservoir and see what we can come up with to share, to give and to receive the blessings that come here forth.

Empathy and Energy in a leader entails knowing how decisions and policy affect people in the organization. It is not reaching goals by stepping on other people's feelings. It is not about enquiring about the families of the team alone, or having barbeques. Sometimes being popular is mixed with being empathic. It is seeing issues from other people's shoes so clarity and perspectives become apparent, and non-issues are not made into issues. Communication is key to removing misunderstandings, silos and negative silence just builds upon anxieties marring what was once good but is not viewed this now.

True empathy arises from the depths of character, understanding, feeling the world from another's shoes. I remember one 'Management Seminar' that I was conducting for the office staff in South India. The office staff were so fed up with being entrusted with the boss's personal work, and having little time left to do their own office work, that they spilled it all out. There was unanimity in the complaints, issues brought up and resolutions sought. The boss was not aware of this. She was riding the high horse of being the boss. Energy flow was affected in the team and there was frustration in the boss. Yet, on the outside everyone smiled and said, 'Hello, how are you?'

It is at these seminars and workshops that truth descends. This is because there is someone to hear their stories, to work with groups and through discussions people come up with solutions alternatives and there is a recharge of battery.

Groups that are successful have leaders whose energy calibrates at a high level and groups that are not have incredibly low calibrating energy. Energy pills and high performance drugs do not do it. The internal element of empathy does it. Changing lenses, seeing other perspectives, feeling another's pain, loss, expectations and endeavouring to keep commitments does it. The leader must be able to inspire, trust and invest in people. His influence must extend beyond the immediate.

Affinity and Adjustability: Affinity is a much misunderstood word. While the dictionary meaning of it is a relationship with a strong liking, similarity, agreeability. *How does this play in a leader's life?* It works at two levels. One it makes him a dear and others work better with him. To have affinity or spontaneity the leader must be authentic and truthful to himself and another. He must not vacillate 'Say one thing do another'. Hip hop dance troubles and takes away from the persona of the leader. It may be interesting at one level – building unpredictability and mystery and keeping another guessing, but when it comes to practicality certainty and specifics are needed.

Affinity requires adjustability in the long run. To keep the passions brewing, and momentum in place, the leader must adjust as much if not more, to the ones he wants to adjust to him and his policies. Leaders are mini managers, but their task goes beyond that of a manager. They are role models, they know what to do, how to deliver truth and transparency and be accountable.

Innovation and Cooperation: Innovation is a problem solving technique as much as creating an environment charged with new ideas and creations. It is a way of looking at things and people with the lens of co-operation and empathy. To elicit cooperation, one has to provide the assistance, the know-how, the tolls to another. Be clear on the path of one's goals and expectations.

Be there for people, be approachable and not an absent leader who works through his private assistants. While this may be necessary in some circumstances, close contact, reciprocity, and accountability go a long farther in building a climate of trust and co-operation.

You will not grow as a leader unless you commit yourself to getting out of your comfort zone. It is only then that teams are built, new learning takes place and initiatives are cooperatively handled and goals reached.

What practices be they spiritual or social will you keep in practice to keep yourself on track? What kind of example will you set? Make today count and tomorrow will look after itself. An invitation to lead people is an invitation to make a difference in both their and your life. It is potential developing in both the self and the other. You can limit your people under the umbrella of fear- appropriate and inappropriate; so, they are afraid to try the new, express themselves for fear of being out of your good books by speaking their mind. Or you can liberate them by open and candid two way communication.

Innovation begins in the middle of conflict and challenges creative solutions to best address problem solving. It is another way of doing things, so people co-operate and join hands. This keeps the grapevine at bay and gets things moving, gets people moving. It is humanistic and productive. It is also a risk and requires courage and conviction. It is not inflexible nor in a fixated trench but open to suggestion alteration and change.

One of the issues with leadership is as we go, so do the people, we lead go. We set the precedent, the path and determine by example the nuances, the road ahead. It begins with being a parent, imbibing. Monkey see, monkey do.

Perceptions, Perspectives and Priorities: The artist paints with his mind and the leader leads with his. It is what the artist sees and how he sees it that makes the painting. Similarly, a judicious leader is discerning. He has a vision and looks for meaning and purpose in his position. His journey is not dependent upon another's approval or disapproval. When the Spirit rises, it can neither be measured nor assessed. Leadership begins early in life. It is a feeling of responsibility, humanity, and dexterity. Positions are reached or not reached later in life. Leadership is the seat of the Spirit. Its sinews are the mind and the heart. It is transformational, relational, transactional, and nimble. I have chosen the lenses of varying kinds of leadership and explored experientially perceptions of different styles and their outcomes. Democracy is not a theoretical term but has practical implications in daily life. We often subject it to the realm of politics, education, business, medicine, and daily interactions. We begin to justify our busyness and non-responsive behaviours, delegating them to secretaries. They listen because they want to oblige, even when they are asked to do something beyond their jurisdiction. Similarly, leaders holding positions want to appear strong, not weak. They continue on the path of proving themselves right to appear strong. Leadership sometimes becomes a game of appearances. Falsehoods creep in.

My observations and experiences have seen leadership doled out as hegemony, denial, rhetoric, belittling and ignoring the vulnerable. Yet, leadership to me is the radiant streak of light that dispels shadows of darkness, sorrow, and makes clear the path that is bestowed on the leader. It resides in the hearts of men and women as much as in their minds and sinews. It is humility in all its aspects. Hence, I call it 'Leadership Service'. The word is self- explanatory. If you wish to serve you choose this path. If you wish to be a singular decision maker and do willy-nilly subscribing to reasons best suited to yourself, and act not out of a moral imperative, there is some pattern that needs to be examined.

CHAPTER THREE

DIFFERENT KINDS OF LEADERSHIP

Leadership is never purely of one type. It is often hybrid. The leader's inherent personality traits come to bear upon his style. A few leadership styles that come to light are:

Affirmative Leader is one who transfers positive emotions, motivation, and inspiration to his team instead of fear of dominance and dictatorship. He is also effective.

Autocratic Leadership is *Authoritarian* leadership when there is singular assumptive decision making. The latter implements his singular choices and communication gets flawed. *Tasks are completed but how and with what kind of fearful energy?*

Charismatic Leadership *is inspirational* and transformational – it requires high productivity from team e.g., Walt Disney – **Nimble Leadership** – walking the line between creativity and chaos. Leadership is seen as coaching to lift people up; not to drag them to the inane. To bring the best out of them not the worst. Leaders train others to be leaders. As it happens most of them put other people's morals down because of their own deficits and incapability in handling situations that are self-created. Most keep making the same mistake over and over again and do not learn from them. This is because they have closed their minds to anything beyond their parochial lens. In doing so they become like frogs in the well who feel the well is the world till they jump out and see it otherwise. Unfortunately, realization comes late in life if at all and has to be brought to their attention by someone close. And when it is they desert that other for her candour and go on as if the person never existed. This is commodification of the human in another. It is a mark of immaturity in the leader.

Nimble Leadership *walks the line between creativity and chaos*. It is a leadership culture that is empowering, accords creative freedom and responds quickly to changes in the business, education cultural or political climate. It is not a command culture but a nurturing one based on coaching and training of its team to perform better and take on positions. The buzz word here is 'innovative'. Knowing that command culture cannot last for long, and change is the name of the game, nimble leadership is looked at favourably. It is not, however, without its downside. While it is enabling at one level, it is also seen as laissez faire or weak by others where everyone does as he or she pleases. There is a lot of latitude and work is delayed.

Democratic Relationship happens when employees are a part of the management, production, policy making and executing and partners in the organization. They choose their own work board, have flexibility a mechanism that allows this freedom. It also balances energies and brings forth entrepreneurs, willingness, and self-confidence. Most of all it brings forth a strategic mindset. Absorbing cultural norms becomes a part of the strategic mindset. Job autonomy brings product development, be it an education program, a cultural shift, a business idea or more.

The stepping up to the plate leadership strategy helps people do more with less. There is spontaneity and willingness to meet the needs of the hour regardless of resources because it is their idea. Ownership fosters responsibility. The process is founded with humility, respect, and feedback with everybody in mind. Not to say that there are no creative collisions. Leaders spot structural holes that need to be filled. They connect the entrepreneur to the customer. This ensures better quality of the product, of delivery and sustainability in business.

"Effective Leadership is not based on being clever; it is based on being consistent." Peter Drucker

Moral Leadership: This is based upon integrity. Gandhi, Roosevelt, George Washington are examples of great leadership. They always had a moral anchor point.

Every leader needs a role model. Success lies in the leader's ability to broker collaborative relationships. In doing so he forges an ecosystem vision. This helps him understand his role in the system, and not get swept away by the power the position holds.

Leadership is role play from a relational not a positional angle. It mitigates differences and cuts through power brokers.

COMMUNICATION

Effective communication is the master key that opens every lock
Good leaders are good communicators.

COMMUNICATION is both positive and negative. To enforce positive results, we must keep the communication open, fluid and two-way. Communication can be open ended or closed door. It is not order giving or order taking but much more. It is that smile that puts a lot of things at ease. It is a two way street and listening prior to speaking helps the leader modulate and monitor his talk according to where the listener is posited.

*Good communication creates **momentum.*** This empowers the leader to initiate and execute tasks with relative ease. Those who procrastinate communication create an abyss where even the most swift ships sink. Without momentum everything seems a load to carry and spanners of discomfort, restrict one's way. It is better not to try to fix issues but to spend time gaining momentum. Momentum is everything in sales, policy execution, creation of values, forces, energizing teams and getting things done in a happy way.

There are momentum makers, momentum breakers and Momentum takers.

Momentum Makers are those who are creative and productive people who make things happen. There is a dearth of these, if you find them keep them.

Momentum Breakers are problem creators, and they bring down the morale of the momentum.

Momentum Takers are there for a good time. They are called those who are there for a ride and good times. They are not dependable but go where the sun shines- fair weather friends.

It is not what leaders make happen, but also what happens to the leaders during the communication process that is vital to establishing the climate of the interaction, relationship, and its results. This is where DNA and upbringing, patterns and re-actions based on them play a vital role in the making or breaking of a leader.

Seldom are leaders seen as people with flaws, compulsions. They are looked up to and expectations surround them. It is humanly impossible to meet all of them. It is possible to take these into account while delivering an address, dealing with people, flogging them, making them invisible or closing doors at them. Communication is closed or open. This decides the fate of the leader as much as that of the recipient. A mature leader has an open mind and a welcoming heart. He does not ghost people. By this I mean he does not fall into negative silence, or bizarre rage. He responds not re-acts a pattern. His amazing relationships do not end in 'you are not welcome' silence. He is above and beyond these. He reciprocates gifts of time and energy as well as those of gratitude. He does not have an entitlement mentality from which he operates. There is humility not arrogance in his demeanour, and this does not change with the tide of time.

CHAPTER FOUR

POSITIONAL LEADERSHIP

Positional Leadership focuses more on the position than what it demands. I remember the broad smiles that welcome some leaders. The Aha moments, the openness the willingness to do anything. It is the moment, the energy and spontaneity that makes for momentum. These cannot be traded by policy recitations; theory nor be brushed aside. Personality has a role to play, but it is authenticity that drives charisma.

Persona, personality, and character play an important role in forming a leader. He builds on strengths and comprehends weaknesses both his and others he works with and assigns portfolios accordingly. Transformational leadership turns every transaction into a transformation by leading with the 'Principle of Truth', inclusiveness, recognition, and forgiveness. While principles are universal, their interpretation is diverse and personal. So is their implementation. To achieve anything, we must strive and get out of our comfort zone.

Leaders often get used to playing power games. These involve intimidation, manipulation, and Silos. When they do this, they may gain momentary power, but they lose influence. They can belittle another by not taking cognizance of them, not responding, show attitude and more. All these traits are ego based. They emanate from hegemony. Temporal power is addictive. It is ephemeral and transient. It shows its negative effect on both the leader and the receiver. Both feel vanquished eventually. The climate of an organization is determined by the Spirit, the demeanour, and the language of communication. Response builds responsibility. Responding to all, even those down in the rung of the hierarchal ladder is Humility. It mitigates fear and anxiety.

Positional Leadership focuses on the importance, dimension, range, of the position and strikes out before it strikes in to observe the inner landscape. It is a mirroring exercise. Positional leaders are insecure and hold on to their positions tightly, lest they lose them. Locked in fear, they seldom feel the breeze, touch the shore, or kiss the dew drops and see them melt. Starched and stiff in their decisions, assumptions, and anxieties they become tin soldiers who march the lines and whine and get stuck in their positional power that negates the other, if they do not get their way.

How they are seen is another matter. Sycophants buzz around them. People are afraid when controlled. There is apprehension and this leads to bringing down openness, candour, and productivity. The leader needs to develop himself by associating with people who help him think and feel authentically. These people should not be those working with him for biases come in. Someone who is a deep thinker and feels for the leader is a good fit. It makes the positional leader perceive with a different lens and be aware of perspective other than him. It loosens him and adds humour and a light step to the heavy tread. There are no hard and fast rules, but the leader makes them up as he or she goes along. It is incumbent upon the leader to place things in context, to prioritize and respond to those who wait for answers.

Positional leaders get glued to their positions and define lines and boundaries for those on the other side of the fence. As a result, open communication suffers. People are afraid to speak their minds and seldom do so as not to be in the bad books of the leader. The positional leader has many expectations, some he voices others he is silent about. Nonetheless there are expectations of the appropriate or inappropriate. He seldom judges openly. It is not done. But he judges secretly and applies his assessments to giving bonuses, portfolios and other. Politeness is the wrap with which he deals with those who offend his sensibilities or those he wishes to keep at bay as his position is important to him. He does not wish to be compromised. Expect expectations, adulation, and sycophancy. Look for meaning in each relationship. *Can it outlive the position? Is it seeking a favour?* Look for truth, candid feedback and cultivate and encourage those who have nothing to gain from you. They would be your true friends. Put time into people and earn their loyalty.

It is more important to make the position than to let the position make you. This is a character-building exercise truly. Here vision and values are tested. The three prime values being: Ethical- Relational- and Success values. These can be interpreted in many ways, but the crux of it all is Faith, commitment, and courage. **Hard core and hard earned.**

OBJECTIFICATION OF PEOPLE BY POSITIONAL LEADERSHIP: They often treat subordinates as cogs in the wheel, to be dispensed with at will. This creates a lack of inconsistency and brings down morale. They ignore many aspects of leading humans by ignoring feelings. Hence, it becomes unilateral leadership. Leadership is about working with, for and alongside people. 'Positional Leadership' relies on control not contribution, says John D.C. Maxwell. Expanding and defending their turf seems to be a priority for them. Others follow examples. These rights are valued more than responsibilities. Territory over teamwork Changing focus to maturity instead of entitlement helps bring power not control to the leader. Positional leadership is lonely because it feels insecure and threatened. This is because of the negative environment created by people feeling undermined.

Leaders are readers of both books and people. In high context culture like Japan, people read the air, India they feel the vibes and China the unspoken is interpreted. Seldom is judgement issued prior to learning about the other person. Nor is a decision made based on assumptions. But yes, communication is different in low context and high context cultures. This is apparent to immigrants who had to learn the nuances of other cultures. Here sensitivity training includes cultural training. Knowing oneself is not quick learning. It takes time and effort and there are many pitfalls. If one has humour it helps, If not cultivating wit and humour assists in meeting and grappling with situations that could turn out unpleasant of it were not taking the light side bringing a laugh and letting them go.

However, position is often misunderstood as power. It is addictive. Position is not power and vice versa. True leadership is not about the position, the control, the decisions singularly made, the assumptions or power. It is about learning a new dimension, a new idea and implementing it. It is about finding a place of service and using it effectively. It is an opportunity to be your best and showcase your best. It strikes an image of control over people and events. People aspire for this coveted position and once they get it, they are reluctant to leave it. **The seat is invisibly glued.** Getting stuck in it is the worst thing that can happen. Yet, it happens. Because a sense of belonging to and becoming the seat inhabits the leader. The more time she spends in it the more she gets accustomed to its tenets. People use positional leadership style to wield power. They objectify people by demeaning them. They become discardable goods at the mercy of the leader's likes and dislikes. This makes people wistful. It makes the leader lonely, stranded and disenchanted. It is better to be alongside, than at the top of the team. There is company here.

As we have seen in both politics and corporations, the **'turnover is high'** if leadership is position oriented. It is simpler to get to the top but harder to keep oneself there. Uneasy lies the head that wears a crown. It is more work than fun. Pinnacle leadership sets an even tone. If he is enthusiastic the team is too, and vice versa. It is not good enough to be physically present. Mental presence and engagement are necessary to achieve goals and maintain relationships.

Making most of one's position is realizing the opportunities to excel as a team. The measure is how the team, not the leader, can realize their potential. The leader becomes a facilitator, a guide an inspiration.

Entitlement is replaced by movement, and skills come into play instead of position. Much of leadership is about encouragement and is inspirational. Leaders give and receive feedback. They do not take anything for granted knowing that leadership is earned and learned in order for it to be established. Socrates said, let he who wishes to move the world, first move himself. Hence role modelling and being exemplary is key.

Leader sets a precedent by his responses, reactions, actions, initiative, and the way he conducts himself. This sets the tone. People are left feeling, "What on earth was their mistake?" In the atmosphere he creates, he may hold on to his position till his tenure ends, or be whisked out. The unfortunate ones are those who for want of better jobs, or for financial needs must bear with injustices thrown at them. All this is done silently. Many a leader uses surrogates to interface him, scapegoats to cover for him, and silent treatment as a ghosting and evading technique. Positional leaders focus on 'Rights over Responsibilities' to safeguard their positions, when they are not really their positions, but the positions they occupy. The attachment to the seat, the becoming of it, is the danger zone. Here ego holds sway and brings the leader down. It affects positive thinking, creates animosity and reduces spontaneity.

While a position is given to people who show potential, it also means self-development. Leaders who do not focus on self improvement do themselves and their organizations a great disservice. Those who feel they have arrived, and everyone should listen to them are on a self-destructive curve. There is always a lot to learn in any given situation for an adult as well as a child. The sooner it is realized the better it is. Leaders come with their perceptions, others with theirs. There is seldom singularity, just stress. Hence open and trustworthy communication is essential. This arises out of humility not attitude.

While aptitude is God given, attitude is not. Gratitude is the answer in each situation. Practicing it brings forth better results. In this coveted position there are as many pitfalls as there are adulations. In spreading the wings of control and power the position becomes the persona and the person the position. Personality cult sets in. Here lies the trouble. It becomes parochial. Decisions become singular. Sycophants surround one and please one. They get promoted. Individuals take over the collective, Care is thrown to the winds. In this lies danger of pitfalls. They come from being power drunk, thinking oneself to be indispensable, assumptions, singular decisions and more.

People who rely on their positions to get things done are weak leaders. They procrastinate their task and defer them, delegating to others serving them. People who work for positional leaders may have independence and proactivity as their traits but soon these diminish, as they come under the positional regime and become subservient to the boss. Boss rules, decides, allocates, determines and others become puppies wagging their tales. If there is any asking from the proletariat is a simple formality. The team knows it. They also know the consequences of not being favoured, losing ground, being ignored and so on.

As a result, those who work under positional leadership become clock watchers. Evaluating time and productivity they look for the time to go home. It becomes a rights culture. They do what they must and no more. They say, "Enough is enough" and make their way out. Dissent has its consequences. The leader's moods and decisions become the finality of situations. There is little compromise other than being compromised.

Leaders have been followers at some time. What they had to deal with plays out now. Subservient impressions, experiences and attitudes take shape unconsciously. Creative use of minimizing tasks and holding off extra time are sought. Time becomes the measuring tape. People become robotic to some degree. The tape plays. They get used to it. Hegemony sets in. They hold their position tags so does the leader. In this culture of leadership, a lot of mental energy is spent in eliminating tasks. Compliance becomes reluctant. Commitment lags. Their hands may be engaged but their hearts and heads are partially engaged. It is always impersonal, distant, and cold. The strange thing is that the leader is so far removed from this notion that she does not consider it. Blindfolded she leads. Apathy sets in the team. They become less proactive, productive, and participative. In this atmosphere the leader loses steam as energy is diffused, the flow interrupted, and personality takes over productivity.

CORRECTIVE MEASURES: The lens with which positional leadership views the team is as subordinates. This came to my attention when I was doing an office management seminar and workshop at a law school in Pune. Towards the end of the session while doing a quiz and during a Q. and A. participants spoke in one voice about the anxieties caused by the leader constantly demanding their time and energy for personal gain, personal takes, delegating personal stuff to the. The voices were so strong that they seemed to have been holding in this stress for a long time and had no venues to air them. Like a pressure cooker the steam could be felt in the room.

Bring Proactivity by fattening others, not just yourself. Take them into account. Observe before assessing. Judge not as you do not know the circumstance, the perspective of another. Lend a hand, ears, and senses to learn. Leaders are readers. It is never enough. The human mind likes order. This order is of varying types. Order of the objects, tasks on hand, or ordering people to do one's will. There is little democracy in decision making. It is not the major decisions but daily decisions that spell the alphabet of democracy. You do not have to speak your position, act your position to enforce it. These are sure pitfalls. Yes, you can amplify the position by imbuing it with a real sense of service.

SELFISH ATTITUDE: "You are here to help me," subjugates and is top down leadership. This needs to be changed with, "I am here to help you."

DISTANCING: Not allowing people to get close to you, maintaining distance to exert power can be non inclusive and generates a cold and impersonal atmosphere encouraging apathy. This has to change to inclusiveness and getting close to the people to really know them not as names but as real people with their emotions, attributes, strengths and weaknesses.

Power really rests in the team, not the leader. Yet, it is exhibited by the leader in the way he conducts himself, with others, by distancing himself, speaking as he chooses, changing his course to suit himself and taking for granted his team and those not on his team too. This is because behaviour patterns have a way of sinking into the psyche and affecting attitude. Once set, attitude dominates decisions and brings about the leader's downfall.

Blindfolded by this attitude, clairvoyance lags. This diminishes the power of the leader. For clairvoyance to emerge, humility and democratic run of the mill is needed.

Content and form both become partners in effective delivering and following of tasks.

Positional leadership always wants to appear strong. Yet it is insecure, afraid, and anxious. It is human to have weak spots. Everyone has them. Not covering but accepting them is key to identification and addressing these. Keen to hold on to the trimmings some leaders dare not appear weak in thought, speech, or action. They are happy to destroy whatever comes in their way to stay on the top. Alas! This seldom happens. Truth has an uncanny way of escaping.

The journey of leadership takes the person through three phases; to **learn, to earn and to repay**.

Learning is essential to lead better. This helps the climb with knowledge and when applied judiciously turns to wisdom. Those who use learning to guard their turf, get enraged by anything and everything and have hard time letting go of fixations arising out of fixed mind sets and prejudices. If experience spells productivity, they seldom notice this. Caught in a maze of their making they march the lines with baton in hand hoping their follower would do the same, after all they have handed her a basket full of goodies.

Intimidation is a technique of positional leadership: "Do this or else…" It is a form of blackmail to which they have been subjected in their formative years by their seniors, parents, and others. This becomes a pattern they fall into in later years. Raising consciousness, seeing themselves as they are with the help of another who dares to be a true friend and revealing all knowing they will fall out of grace when they do so is a big help for positional leaders. They hear what they choose to and ignore what they choose to. It is personality driven, personal like taking over responsibility. They transfer responsibility and scapegoat those under their power very politely. This is diplomacy in practice in positional leadership and is also called transactional leadership. As this objectifies the other to a number, an object to be toyed with used and discarded. Friendships fall under this preview too.

Positional nee transactional leaders seldom make lasting friends or partners being so caught up in their parochial multiple personalities, they find it hard to throw off the position and be their authentic self. They fall into hierarchical thinking patterns. I am here; you are there. Those who show differences are treated differently – a bias sets in and this is both constrictive and damaging. Positional leaders want control. So they do everything to get it even at the cost of another.

They want to look good, seem right, and in doing so falter and end up creating a situation they were running from. Herein lies the pitfall.

It is my endeavour to raise awareness of followership first and leadership after to show the relationship. Just as the child first and the teacher later. We have been putting the cart before the horse. The Indian way was for the teacher to appear when the student was ready. Respect was ensured. Today respect is gone because the teacher takes little cognizance of the subject- the student. There is an element of inborn traits like humanness to make and admit mistakes in oneself and others, an open mind, a giving heart and willingness to sacrifice which determine the mettle of a leader. This is oft tried in different crucibles.

What comes out is what the raw material of humanity breathes in us. Whether we take a positional stand or a relational stand on the chair we occupy determines our success as both leaders and humans. The seat does not determine the person. The person determines the seat. Those who sacrifice personhood to the seat, play the dictums of the seat. In their minds they may be doing great. They become a boss not a leader. Relational leadership goes through the throes, the slings, and arrows to come out unscathed in serving with humility.

How much of positional leadership is personality based? Celebrity culture of today has taken the steam off the essentials and used cosmetic forms of leadership styles to thwart what is important. In the glamour of lights and camera much is lost. Leadership is not hierarchical but complimentary. Leaders who are narcissists are an end in themselves. There is a moral imperative to every decision as it impacts others. When in a position of power sometimes leaders impact others negatively by their decisions. Leadership is a bittersweet journey into an unknown land with no destination in view. It involves change.

Positional Leaders expect their subordinates to run the course of events, do the hard work. This weakens not strengthens them as they lose the personal touch with those they govern. Reality becomes their assumption and truth seldom reaches them through the walls of sycophancy. Their employees turn out to be 'just enough' types, doing only what is required of them. They may give their hands but not their heads and hearts. There are people who, though physically present, are really not there mentally. Lack of mental engagement costs the organization of initiative. The result is mediocrity. Positional leadership just gets by, lacking in creativity and innovation.

The longer the positional leaders stay in their positions, the harder it gets for people to change their perceptions about them. Unless of course they dramatically change their manner of operation and walk alongside their people not above or below them. Partnership, acquiescence, and vulnerability that come from risk taking are needed to do so. Sitting in one's comfort zone does not get one any further. It gets uncomfortable after a while. Positional leadership becomes lonely when beset with fears and apprehensions of losing image, appearing weak, coming too close, being found out or being transparent.

EXAMPLES OF POSITIONAL LEADERSHIP

Positional leadership comes from the position held and is not necessarily based in integrity.

Some examples of Command Culture: 'My way or the Highway' mentality. 'Know your place'. 'You dare not disobey'. 'Do as I say not as I do'. 'You are here to serve'. 'I will tell you what to do'. These are some subconscious thoughts and perceptions like these surface when a positional leader takes power. It becomes a force not true power. Insecurity and Fear set in. Decisions are singular and assumptive. People are afraid to dissent. There are implications, supplications, and a negative atmosphere. Morale is low. Intent is high. Clock watchers emerge. Many change jobs. Those who stay become stupefied, cease growing. They never know what is right other than what the leader tells them to do. Independence of thought and speech take a back seat. Me versus you attitude sets in.

It can transport itself to Leadership by Compliance according to the Harvard psychologist Herbert Kelwan. By this he means the leader expecting agreeability despite the disagreement of this team.

Most leaders who have led masses by popular vote try to get their goals met, use mass media to create a worshipful image of a hero. It is often seen in totalitarian or authoritarian states and regimes. This filters through organizations, political, corporate, educational, and personal relations. When this happens, there is danger of the leader becoming a despot and doing away with a relationship that does not suit him. There is no leadership left but despotism rules and anarchy results. History is replete with such examples. This form of leadership is directive in nature as it depends upon giving directions for others to follow leaving little room for initiative or open ended questions. It is transactional in nature as the leader rewards or punishes those who work under him by their level of agreeability with him. Rewards could be a promotion, financial, getting to do a course that develops potential or being in the inner circle and having an in with the leader. It has a quantitative approach to getting results.

Relationship building is a two-way process. People grow with each other as much as towards each other. These dynamics come into play in marriage as much as at work. You establish the relationship – then you abandon it. Divorce is not a piece of paper, nor is lay off at work. Both arise out of handling relationships improperly. There is always work to do for the leader. Those leaders who do not acknowledge this do themselves and their teams or another a disfavour. Like moody teenagers they swing from side to side and never balance their characters, even though they may balance their budgets at someone else's costs.

Building relationships with people is a continuum. A leader must be consistent and able to stay his word and risk his temperament for it. Sacrifice for the sake of a vision for yourself and your team. You do not sacrifice relationships but personal comfort zones. Connect to people's potential not to let them down and say "enough is enough". Maturing is mellowing.

CHAPTER FIVE

RELATIONAL LEADERSHIP

Relational leaders focus on developing harmonious relations by shifting the focus from 'me' to 'us'. Chemistry develops in the team, and it feels more like a family. The 'have to' mind set, changes to 'want to' mindset. More energy is brewed at work. The attitude prevailing is one of helping each other and allowing for collective endeavour where one person's success is also another's success too. Rivalry and jealousy take a back seat. They take the team to higher levels of energy, called 'synergy'. They prepare tomorrows leaders while in their seats. This is the pinnacle of leadership.

When you spend time cultivating relationships, they become pillars of strength, you can lean on and trust in real time when the going gets rough and when you really need to trust people to carry on beyond you. Relationship culture is built by conversations in real time. Uncertainty, stress, anxiety, apprehensions and saying something they never meant to that will mar their image, keeps leaders from connecting authentically. When bosses close the door so they can speak to you freely and you to them, they are feeding fears and using these to protect what they fear. The Grapevine.

You may have eight cylinders in an organization but how many are really firing? You may have ten within you, yet there is reluctance and reservation in firing even half of them. It is easier for some leaders to fire people than to fire their enthusiasm or motivation, to connect, clear and commit. Creating a culture of innovation requires a white board where you can list all that is culture. Being so amorphous you will be surprised by the definitions and broad dimensions of culture. Culture is not the sum of personalities. It does not just happen as commonly thought. Yet, it drives results, motivation understanding and initiative. It is the backbone of every organization and its engine. *Why do we give so little importance to it and just let it happen?* A company's culture is more important than its strategy because it leads the way, it is the way, and it determines the way.

The biggest problem that organizations face in creating a company culture is fear of forming silos, tribes within the big tribe of the organization. These compete with each other and instead of fighting competition outside they fight amongst themselves for power and prestige, much is lost, and little is gained. In today's tech world many people spend most of their time sitting behind their 30-inch screens. There is little human contact. This affects the neurotransmitters adversely, so it hampers connectivity and results. What you can achieve in face-to-face conversation you cannot in a hundred emails which are transaction not relational. They speak through another mouth where language gets distorted and there is no instant feedback. No reading of body language. No reading the air as the Japanese call it.

Communication is the key to problem solving and non communication to creating problems. This is the truth. Many heartaches and lives could be saved by simple and clear communication. Yet, this does not happen. The reason seems to be ego. Inability to face another's truth, wanting to have one's way, being misled by Chinese whispers, getting side-tracked by opinions and patterns of behaviour. *When there is so much on the table, where and how does anyone bring peace and prosperity to the table?* The answer lies in the abundance mentality. In fostering a feeling of acceptance of another as he or she is, by non judgemental attitudes and making allowances. This is not weakness but a strength. IT is the language of humanity many never learn to speak. Mission statements stay in binders. Living the life of a Christian and being a Christian are two quite different credos. Same applies to all religions, creeds, and companies. If every employee is the signature of the company reflecting its values, it is time to discuss demeanour not with the measuring stick of what is appropriate and what is not but with the stick of comprehending another. Enforcing our will and opinion on another does not resolve but creates problems. Understanding perspectives of others teaches us more about them.

Leadership is not a manual but a mechanism.

Relational leadership transforms the individual and then the organization hence, it is also called transformational Leadership. It enhances the relationship between the leader and his team by building a Trust between them. This is the base on which we function. It allows for dependability, consistency, and predictability. It is also important for creating a responsible environment. It asks the questions:

Have I invested enough in this relationship that allows me to be candid with the person concerned? Do I value the relationship, or the transaction suited to me? Is it her issue or really mine? Am I intimidating or being intimidated and is this the reason for creating the situation I find myself in? Is the issue more important than the relationship? Does this conversation serve both or is singular and self serving? Am I willing to invest time, energy, and resources in helping the person concerned change? What will I achieve and for who, by deciding what I am going to do?

The term 'Relational' was proposed first by Hollander in 1958. It has two components. One is inclusiveness; it views leadership as a social construct. It takes the focus off the position and makes leadership people oriented. From a command culture it turns leadership to inspirational culture. Leadership is not a male quality as was deemed in the past. James MacGregor Burns, a leadership expert, first proposed this theory. There are **four different components** of this theory according to Burns who advanced it. These are:

- It be intellectually Stimulating
- It be Supportive and Inspirational
- It motivate by Appreciation
- It bring forth loyalty and be effective

Performance improves when these components are made inherent to leadership. People feel empowered. Trust, passion, and energy levels are high as giving and receiving feedback become means of improving oneself. This helps combat misunderstandings, fatigue, and adds meaning to work. Effective communication skills are the backbone of transformational or Relational Leadership. Communication is both verbal and nonverbal. Sometimes gestures, facial expressions, negative silence say more than words do. It can dampen enthusiasm and destroy initiative. The leader must be aware of the involuntary muscles of his face that move to a 'yes' or a 'no' quickly. These can be read as value judgements of the person concerned. Putting down someone never helped, Manipulating by speaking from two sides of the mouth is not diplomacy though it is project to be. It may accomplish short term gaols and be a band aid but eventually it makes both the person who hands those out and the person to who it is handed suffer. In this form of leadership, the leader seeks permission of the group before making decisions, advancing tasks, giving orders, gifting, or other. He acts in an inclusive not assumptive way. Once they agree he has their consent to move forward. Thus, acquiescence is received, and everyone is on board. When a situation that requires candid speaking comes forth: it must be addressed quickly before **procrastination builds enmity**. It must be privately addressed to save both faces. The tone is calm and cordial. It is not the person you are attacking but the policy.

Candidness is a two-way street. Allow another to be candid and be accepting of it just as you wish to be candid and accepted. Maturity to take feedback or suggestions without being defensive or personally, assists in maintaining and strengthening relationships. We do not want sycophants but friends. Soliciting feedback is maturity. **Compromise is a constant need**. It cannot be measured. Anyone who has been in a long-term relationship knows that. It is not my way or the highway. Gratitude and kindness are the companions of compromise. While businesses may value contribution over family, families value community over contribution. Balance between the two is not being compromised fully, and not compromising another.

Quick on their heels are responsibility and accountability of actions, words, and deeds. In your privileged position as a leader, it is hard but necessary to strike a balance between candour and care for another. Responsibility is not to be delegated nor shirked without accountability. When this is done it becomes a passing the buck game. This diminishes both and the larger picture is affected adversely. Loyalty gets compromised. Initiative gets affected and the grape vine activates falsehoods.

First, we start by breaking barriers in communication and being **approachable and available**. This is the ice breaker. Relationships can be meaningful or meaningless. We get attracted to meaningful relationships as they help us grow, validate us, and we see the road ahead. This road is not necessarily goal oriented, but it is enriching. It reaffirms our faith in us and in another. These people come into our lives and show us the way. We see ourselves from their eyes. A new me emerges. I never knew it existed. But by the presence of another in our lives we form, reform, or deform. This is what relationships do.

It is not only important to grow towards each other but to grow together towards developing potential, advancing vision and living values. When we do not grow together, we fall apart. **Sustainability** of a leader depends upon taking the people with him. Relational side of leadership does not end with asking about our welfare, families etc. It is a perennial task. It involves risk taking, gumption, nerves, courage to stand up and vulnerability to travel the road less travelled. Relationships never reside in comfort zones. Fair weather friendships do. They dwindle when the weather gets rough. Building relationships precedes allocating tasks, or asking people to do something, comply, follow you. Leaders are the eyes, heart, head, and sinews of the company. They show that with the attitude of care they adopt.

Good leaders are **proactive** and reach results. They do not do this singularly but in cohesion with the team. They create an environment of success by fostering a congenial climate of trust. This is built brick by brick. It can, however, be hammered down with one axe. To avoid this from happening consideration for another, taking another perspective into account, establishing a personal relationship not distancing oneself helps. It speaks the language of humanity.

Momentum develops and the team performs better. *There are momentum makers, momentum takers and momentum breakers.* Momentum makers are those with fresh ideas, steam, and enthusiasm to implement them. Momentum takers are these the leaders need to energize to act for the entire team to work together. They usually go along for the ride. Momentum breakers are those who hurt morale by finding something negative to complain and fret about. Like a wet blanket they bring the energy down. If momentum breakers after given a chance to rise to the occasion and pitch in do not perform, they better be moved to another slot, or the entire team will gradually get affected adversely.

The key to building the best team is recognizing those who are there for the ride and those who are prepared to sacrifice and stay, to be proactive and make things happen. The cost of leadership is responsibility. "Success is an uphill journey". Staying along the shore you do not always catch fish, sometimes you must swim into the waters and feel the temperature, dive and feel the waters. This is experiential leadership. We establish relationships when we care for people genuinely. We build trust. We expand the relationship when we are candid with them. Instead of fear for being candid and being rebuked, ignored, or slighted, we show trust and acceptance of dissenting parties. In doing so, we get another perspective and agree to disagree but do not lose the relationship

There will be moments when you tire, get disenchanted and wish you had more time to yourself. In these moments you need to take a break from yourself and your feelings. Leadership is not closing one door at someone and opening another for someone else. It is a continuity. Relationships because of a burn out in you is dismantling all you stand for. It disintegrates the personality and goes against one's grain. **Integrity speaks the language of continuity, not closure**. Do whatever it takes to keep from losing the trust that is bestowed on you and you have achieved over the years.

Understand how your personal gifts contribute to relationship building. These gifts may be abilities, understanding, complementing, appreciating, a positive stroke or a thankyou gesture in the form of a gift. *Best behaviours are not outwardly immaculate but inwardly sound.* They do not demean another, demarcate, distinguish, and include others. This may seem hard but with practice it becomes easy, and even fun as one does not feel alone in the shadows and in the dark. It is an emotional rejuvenation of the team. This has been my experience.

EXAMPLES OF RELATIONAL LEADERSHIP

Caring should never suppress candour and vice versa. People think that if you care for people, you will always agree with them. This is unnatural, as each one of us is different. Good Leadership means being responsible for one another and disagreeing to agree. This simple dictum is often forgotten by autocratic leaders who want everyone to do as they command and toe the line; there is no room for dissenting voices. As such they surround themselves with sycophants not real friends. Fair weather friends flock to their sides. Each has a motive, and the leader rewards them for their compliance, not for what they contribute to his growth. This does not benefit the leader. Like the emperor with no clothes he lives in an illusory world.

THE CARING AND CANDOUR CHECKLIST

Trust is enough for being frank. Latter is speaking your truth. It does not have to be obligatory for another to comply.

1. *Do you value this person enough to be forthright?*
2. Do not speak up for personal reasons like being threatened.
3. The issue should never be more important than the relationship.
4. Do not create situations that will come to haunt you or destroy the relationship, making it a fight or flight response.
5. *Are you willing to invest time, energy and*

resources in the relationship or just stay in your comfort zone with what is familiar and pleasant? Growth needs stepping outside the comfort zone.
6. *Is the criticism creative and constructive or destructive and demeaning? Does it help the other person grow and change for the better? Does it show another way of doing things that is more productive?*
7. *Are you setting clear expectations, both for yourself and the other?*

POINTS TO CONSIDER:

1. Be spontaneous in your response. This does not mean do not reflect. It means answer promptly as silence and delay is often misunderstood.

2. Respond from a place of calm, not rage. If you feel rage express, it without insults.

3. Candid speaking comes from open mindedness. It does not embarrass nor belittle another.

4. Candour is a two-way street. Allow another to be candid with you as you are with her. Show maturity in accepting differences. Space is not silence. It is comprehending and accepting another for who or what they are.

CARING ESTABLISHES RELATIONSHIPS CANDOUR EXPANDS THEM

While chemistry and thought patterns create ambivalence, they do not expand a relationship as open mindedness does. Parachutes, they say work best when open. So do our minds and our relationships. Conversations turn to silo to avoid difficulties in expressing what one truly feels or how one honestly thinks. This keeps one restricted to a parochial perspective. When two sides of the coin are seen, decisions and perceptions enlarge. This prevents misunderstandings and clears the air. Communication becomes easier and candid. Two reasons like confrontation and avoiding hurting another keep one from expressing oneself truly. Often, what one fears happens. People may shut down with candour, but they have not shut down permanently. You have reached their essential self. Caring may **define** a relationship and candour may **direct** it. Both have a role to play. To move together caring and candour must neither **replace** nor **displace** one another. Each has a place and each needs attention, balance, and time to sort itself out. Caring values the person and candour the potential the person has. Both are critical to effective leadership.

Being productive does not always translate into being a good leader. One can be a good producer yet, not a good leader. Personal success is not team success. Necessarily. "Leadership is defined by what a person does for the others". Those who shirk responsibility and delegate it to subordinates to avoid facing the music are never good leaders. They run their campaign by proxy. There is nothing like face to face interrelatedness generated by live connection. Substitutes are simply that and cannot achieve the result that an effective leader can.

Each of the alphabets in the word 'Effective' is a domain in itself. It has a positive effect on the people, the organization, and the leader. It is rigour, respect, rancour, and reliance. *How can one person achieve this singly?* The answer is "no she cannot." To expect the unexpected, the impossible is not what we are talking about. Effectiveness is a combination of empathy, fortitude, forthrightness, energy. Fuzzy thinking brings unclear visions and execution. This topples values of trust and accountability. On the other hand, a compelling vision is clear and well defined. It covers all areas and is succinct in definition. It is aligned with the team's values. Most importantly it energizes the team because it is democratic.

Effective leaders help the team realize the value of vision, define it together, discuss it, debate it, demarcate its scope and execution policy. They know the challenges and make a map of how to meet these as they arise. They also allow space for spontaneity, creativity, clarity, and errors. The commitment of the team begins with the leader's commitment, so committing to the team is step one. Gaining credibility and confidence come with commitment and courage of one's conviction. A vacillating leader ignores the moral imperative of his decisions and the ripple effect it produces on others.

An effective leader helps people feel good about their success and inspires them. Developing a team requires insight into each player and building an atmosphere of camaraderie and understanding. Human nature being what it is there are bound to be challenges. Defining expectations both ways helps. Probability and possibility charts help. Mapping challenges helps. Realizing potential, creative minds, candour and clarity amongst the team go a long way in making any task easy and success assured. No one is so strong as to ignore the team, nor so weak as not to stand by one's values of courtesy, honesty, and integrity. Recognizing the strength and weakness of the team members helps. Building on their strengths helps more. As they become conscious of their roles and goals, they pattern out their place in the organization. Realization of each one's task must come from the team's members. What is doable and acceptable to them and what is not. It must not be an assumptive and singular decision of the leader or his inner circle. Both can be biased. But the individual knows and will give her best when assigned what is suitable for her, and what she is competent at.

PROGRESS VERSUS PEOPLE: The latter defines relationship leadership. It is not a social construct but a positive way of leading. It is humane and factors in people's weakness, making goals measurable and leaving room for errors. Leaders who are insecure do their utmost not to show it. They cover it with silos, evasion techniques, manipulations, white lies, using buffers and masking. This does not work in the long run. It diminishes their persona. Moreover, it builds anxiety and fear. Relationships get nipped in the bud.

When a leader learns to give more than he gets, he is on the right path. It is then that he shows his calibre and so do others. Giving means time, attention, a listening ear, non judgemental attitude, care, and empathy. It also means admitting when wrong and not being fixated. Humility is the cornerstone of leadership.

Writing a credo of one's beliefs, attitudes and actions, helps the leader stay on track. Effective leaders often feel like Atlas with a hump on his back. This is the hump responsibility. They want to be in complete control of the situation by micromanaging. This does not always work. Though when it does, they are rewarded for the expectations they met. But at what cost? By objectifying the underdogs, ruining their health, increasing everyone's stress levels. The masquerade is not effective. It is detrimental to families and the leader. This disqualifies them from leading and stunts their potential as a leader.

The example of Moses testing the waters of the Red Sea first, is risk-taking with true faith. The Leader takes that chance. He goes first to test the waters and deal with the ambiguities. He does not defer this to another. People follow with an increased chance of completing the journey.

Leaders do not nip relationships but keep developing them. This is their storehouse of strength. They do not allot shelf life to those who work with them. Stay connected to your people and put **Connection Time** on your Schedule.

Let your personal gifts contribute to the vision you carry and share with the team. There is a strong relationship between giftedness and effectiveness. Focus within your talents and see the team's potential rise. Productivity starts with the leader.

When the vision is clear and can factor in the team's talents, focusing on giftedness, it becomes positive and all hurdles are crossed cooperatively. When leaders commit to the success of this vision, they gain credibility and their team gains confidence. Rewarding and appreciating small daily victors help move the target further. They validate people.

FIVE MAIN PORTALS OF EFFECTIVE LEADERSHIP HINGE ON:

1. **Vision:** This must be shared, clear and doable.
2. **Values:** Honesty, Consistency, Integrity, Kindness
3. **Relationships:** Open mindedness, accessibility, Making Time
4. **Attitude, Gratitude and Empathy**
5. **Communication:** Listening and Responding, open ended.

Taking an inventory of these each day keeps the leader on track. He knows where the shoe pinches, where there are loose hinges and clarifies, communicates, and creates a platform for discussion, inputs, a place where people can put their feelings, give their feedback, and express their point of view. This also brings democracy into the domain. IT is helpful for the leader to know all this to be effective, reach goals, achieve, and creates synergy.

It is not good enough to theorize productivity, have zoom meetings enumerating expectations. It is more vital to roll up your sleeves and get down to the brass tacks and deal with the nitty gritty instead having a command culture. I have found this to be very rewarding.

An effective leader is an empowering leader. **He builds trust by trusting first**. He never betrays trust. This is integrity. When I trust people, I put a little piece of myself in your hands. You can honour my trust by trusting me back or dishonour it by putting a shelf life on the relationship. The effective leader is humane.

Holding yourself and people accountable makes them work better towards deadlines. With accountability there are results, without it people tend to drift. Accountability once again starts with the self. To be accountable for one's word, time, talent, duties, agenda and others is no mean task. It needs time management, willingness to commit, to care, not just lip service.

Many centres for 'Organization Skill Development' entail that depending upon a person's ability, tasks should be handed out. The independent person can do the job proactively, without interruptions. He solves the problems on the way and knows how to produce results.

Keeping a steady head on your shoulders is key to staying in power. Remembering the early days when you faced problems similar to those now faced by employees is a good way to empathize. It builds trust. It also prevents the position from defining the leader.

An effective leader plans for has succession. They plan to hand the baton when at their peak performance. They train and mentor people to the role they assign them and expect them to follow after them. Leaders hurt the momentum of an organization by staying too long. Leaving behind a positive legacy means recognizing how our daily demeanour and effort is building a legacy for us in the long run.

Leaders must decide what their legacy would look like, feel like and be. Legacy is not snippets but the sum total of one's life. Regrets are futile. IT is best to make each day count and be ready to leave with a happy heart.

Teachable moments are a result of levers. WE do not learn just because someone out there wants us to. That is why it is when I hurt, that I learn about pain and adversity, when my trust is broken, I learn about fidelity and honesty in relationships. Wise leaders know that people change when they have adequate knowledge and educational experience. They change when they have received enough to support themselves. Every leader must draw upon his or her crucible moments to pass on and help the next generation.

It is important to identify one's crucible moments. First write them down. Then share the stories with others. The feedback may not always be favourable. That should not keep you from sharing.

GIVING EXPOSURE TO THE TEAM: One learns from varied experiences. Exposing the team to interviewing good leaders, having discussions about pitfalls in their tenure helps build bridges of communication. Use your contacts and Access card in society and business to help your team go ahead. Expose them to opportunities. Connect them to possibilities. Change the stance from fuzzy thinking to possibility thinking. Every time you do that you are making a difference in the world, in society.

Leadership is not a popularity contest. It is a probability measure of possibilities that open up by you being on the chair.

Effective leadership makes people feel like stakeholders in the organization, in the relationship in communication. This keeps them from feeling like a stake to be had at pleasure and convenience. Taking their permission increases positivity. The fine line between manipulating and motivating people lies in following the golden rule: "Make them feel at the top of the world sometimes if not all times." I remember three things that leadership told me.

One: A sense of humour. I was in Teachers' College in a Catholic institution. It was co-ed. Next to me sat Clive Burns. His brother Randolph Burns was in the same class. One day Clive got his head shaved and came to class. Everyone stared at him. He was so conscious that he opened the lid of the desk pretending to take books out, and would put it down when no one was looking. Sitting beside him, I could not help noticing the number of times the desk lid was opened and closed.

Sister Agenesia was a stern nun. She took attendance and called out Randolph Burns. No response. Then again… no response. Randolph was not in class. She loudly said: "Clive, where is Randolph?"

Apprehensively, Clive took his head out and said with a straight face: "Sister, Randy is having his monthlies." He said it as a matter of fact and so loudly that the entire class went into splinters of laughter including Sister Agenesia.

She had not expected this answer. None of us had. Clive had a sense of humour. He made light of serious things. Today he is in a leadership position heading an education board in India.

Two: Leaders must be good observers. I remember after a long conversation with Klaus Brumbach not knowing he was the consulate general, I told him how happy I was that he had quizzed me for my psychology exam. I also complimented him on his inputs into the chapter on 'Motivation'.

Three: Bringing home correction in a way that the person corrected sees and understands without being offended is an art and a science. Philip has that. I had to look inwards and examine myself and not blame the other or the situation.

We are the creators of our destiny, our happiness, our sorrow, would say. I understand today, His evergreen words: Stay Positive. Relationships must lead to developing potential else they fritter into pleasantries. Influencing the team, the relationship, taking it a step forward by evolving is the key. It develops potential both theirs and yours. A teacher in a classroom knows this.

In the classroom of life solid relationships are built on shared values. Yet, this is often forgotten. Leadership is not a destination but a journey. It is what a leader says and does and not the title he wears that matters. It is the ability to connect with people at an emotional and relational level. This makes soldiers lay down their lives and brings forth astute loyalty.

Leadership is about asking the right questions, encouraging questions and feedback. The first question an aspiring leader must ask himself is "Why am I here?" An honest answer would direct him to do what he is there to do. When he loses his way, he must ask again: 'What am I doing here?' It will highlight his actions, motivation, and results.

Finally, before leaving the post, he asks: "What did I achieve? Was it congruent with my aspirations? Did I leave a legacy if so, what?"

Finally in the realm of Leadership what counts more than cognition, technical and managerial know how is emotional intelligence. This cannot be bought nor learnt from a book. This is a cultivated art. When choosing a leader, subjective criteria are more important than objective criteria. Degrees may get him in the door, but emotional intelligence keeps him there. Global companies hire psychologists with competency models to measure emotional intelligence. Developing the leader within is a lifetime of self development with far reaching results.

THREE TOOLS IN THE LEADER'S KIT THESE ARE: KNOWING, SHOWING AND GROWING

The leader needs to know his people, show them the way by role modelling and effective communication. Most importantly he needs to grow them by inspiring them, positioning the right person in the right slot, and developing and empowering them, so they are accountable to those who work with them.

I end with the powerful words that I carry in my head at all times:

"Human life has no boundaries, provided it recognizes the wonderful and beautiful potentialities of the individual human being." Alden B. Dow

CHAPTER SIX

POSITIONAL AND RELATIONAL LEADERSHIP

Positional Leaders drive **rights** over **responsibilities**: Their first mantra is safety, security, task oriented ness, people who get in the way are terminated. In many ways this form of leadership is negative. It is one way communication, one way expectations. Our relationships develop though some amazing relationships come by, but they are short lived. Insecure in their seats and image, the leader crosses them before their shelf life to keep a clean image. Often, the opposite happens. This for, of leadership is image driven. It is not honest and does not reward honesty either. It rewards results. Hence, it is Machiavellian in nature. Having a right to do things is not being righteous. The moral imperative is not considered in decision making. Morality does not lie in scriptures alone. It is embedded in humanity and character. Seldom do leadership courses discuss this. Leadership is not power. It is empowering others. When a leader does not do that, he empowers himself. This empowerment is personality and position related and blinds reality. How many leaders grow in their position without depending upon rights to rule relationships? Only when we mature outside of rights mentality, do we grow in a mature way.

Positional leaders create a negative work environment by darning the 'Queen of Sheba' mentality. They put down people of talent by moving away from them, showing them their place, being curt and change in stance. Seldom do these leaders rise to your trust. Transparency is a far cry. They fear their name and place at the top may be threatened. They also get branded and get tagged. Hostility sets in.

Having influence and power is not the same as being powerful and influential. Positional leaders subscribe to the latter. Many competent people leave their jobs because they do not wish to work with autocratic leaders with an entitlement mentality who feel they have no obligation towards another.

People who rely on their positions are weak leaders. Because they give their least, they get the least from their team. They demotivate by demarcating and build on differences.

Power Tactics: These are used as motivation to push and prompt action. They are grouped in three categories:

1. BEHAVIOURAL: The leader's demeanour changes when compliance to his motives, agenda, desires, and decisions is not obtained. Like a chameleon he comes heavy on the noncompliant, independent minded. The narcissist in him feels threatened. He loves sycophants. They keep him from growing. He stays nestled in his beliefs, opinions, comfort zone. It is familiar to him. Getting out of it feels insecure. This he cannot do. So, he tries to replace courage with charisma. Saying one thing and being another. In this duality he does more harm to himself than others. Eventually, the veil of lies lifts. What he struggled to procure, safeguard, and retain loses lustre. He becomes ordinary and is viewed as such. In his orderliness his masks fall, and the persona suffers a decay.

2. RATIONAL: One cannot reason emotion. Yet, putting a lid on it by negative silence, not welcoming questions, changing one's mind according to one's moods, justifying and rationalizing one's decisions are tactics positional leaders apply to meet their ends, decisions, and agenda.

3. STRUCTURAL: Structural Tactics shift from soft to hard tactics like intimidation, to get the results the leader desires. His decisions reign paramount and there is an inflexibility in his approach and mannerism. Often this is done to seek alibis and make scapegoats of another. These behaviours are projections of the leader's unfulfilled desires, anxieties and patterns imbued in his psyche in early childhood and growing years.

In comparison to positional leaders are relational leaders. Their mantra is building on relationships to team and co-operate in endeavours. Relational leaders know they cannot do it alone. Sitting perched on the top may have its advantages of getting a better view of those around, but it does not get friendlier, understanding of one another. It is isolatory. Creativity and change come with relationship building. They can be awesome or not. What matters is if the leader treats them with a shelf life and puts an expiration date on them.

When people are objectified momentum is lost, spirit of leadership stained and the hurts that ensue bear a name: Trust is breached. When relationships are perennial they water the garden of leadership, creating an ambience of joy. Those leaders who turn into wet blankets become a weight carried on the shoulders of those who associate with them. *Whose purpose do they serve?* They are natural learners, listeners and liked for what they do and not the position they are in.

Relational leaders create a leadership culture by being Champions. They role model good leadership, make time and are never busy to converse with. They teach leadership on a regular basis by briefings, meetings, lectures, and example. They know it is human to fail, to make mistakes and do not hold this against people. They are a help to emerging leaders by showing them the way and being available. They coach and reward best practices.

Leadership is a **life commitment** not a job commitment. It goes beyond the boundaries of the office and takes in the highs and lows of the job as one trajectory to travel and repair time and again. Leaders need to meet the needs of the people. And these are many. Raising leadership qualities in the young is a social commitment every parent must make to enhance responsible. Leadership at this calibrated level is a win- win for the organizations it is based on chemistry between people. It has both a quantitative and a qualitative result.

When leadership is exhibited without a title it becomes informal but does not lose its impact upon people. Daniel Goleman writes in his book, *Leadership for Quality and Innovation*, "Influence is not about charm – it is about versatility, adaptability, and accommodating differences."

CHAPTER SEVEN

EFFECTIVE LEADERSHIP

Effective Leadership is a relentless quest for perfection. It is about knowing and doing things collectively. This does not mean one has to be a perfectionist. No. It simply means one must aim for being one's best and aspiring others to do the same. Mediocrity sucks. Yet, it is there, and it brings a lackadaisical attitude to the organization. This makes people without a limp to limp too. It begins with procrastination by the leader. Others follow. The game of procrastination steals time, energy, and initiative. The latter brings **genuine participation** to the fore. It involves giving and receiving feedback. It is inclusive and a creative way to lead. This brings a positive spirit to the workplace mitigating issues of mental health. It does not favour one over the other. It enables and empowers. Power is misunderstood as control. It is influence. The latter makes happy followers. It is judicious and non-judgemental, ethical, and transformational. The challenge is to find the transformative in the transactional and raise the mundane to ethereal. This makes the specific universal, imbuing values into vision and making it a reality.

What does effective leadership look like? Under its banner people are relaxed, have candour and can speak without reservation, knowing they will not be misunderstood. When the leader speaks from two sides of his mouth, he creates confusion in the minds of the people and does not foster trust. In order to gain trust, one must show trust in people. Trust them first to gain their trust. You have nothing to lose by risking your trust and everything to lose by not risking it. The tone of the team depends upon invaluable Trust relationships.

The leader does this by engaging with zest and passion. In order to do this, he must first know himself and cultivate the traits that can be understood, that appeal and are doable. He makes sure of his oars before getting into the water. He does not indulge in blame games, excuses or scenarios that compromise his vision. Instead of shrinking his vision, he raises and enlarges by appreciation an understanding his team's vision.

It is important to make daily 'To Do' and 'Not to Do' lists in the four spheres: **people, tasks, time, and resources**. This keeps the leader on track. It is also important not to bite off more than one can chew, to look after oneself so there is no burn out. I speak from example. When burn out takes place one gets into a rage, and seeks scapegoats, gets irritable and often acts impulsively.

A calm approach to problems and issues one faces needs reflection, meditation, and insights. It is important to choose one's friends carefully. IT is more important to befriend your authentic self, see your warts and all, and self correct. This becomes necessary as one stands with crowds, and alone eventually.

Keeping an **emotional chart** helps the leader know his trigger points. Keeping a psychological chart helps him identify his stress points. To balance the energy Tai Chi be practised and visualization exercises, vipassana mindfulness, chanting of mantras helps.

EFFECTIVE LEADERSHIP INVOLVES:

1. ACTIVE LISTENING: This is the fundamental of gaining knowledge.

2. SELF AWARENESS: This builds vigilance and reflection.

3. INTEGRITY: Consistency, compassion and more knit the personality.

4. EMPATHY: Feeling what the other is feeling is key to understanding.

5. POWERFUL QUESTIONS: Leaders who encourage questions build bridges and solve problems.

6. INTENTIONAL LANGUAGE: Carefully chosen vocabulary to avoid misunderstanding and build rapport is key to harmonious relationships.

7. LEADERSHIP PRESENCE: An absent leader is no leader. He works through proxy and people do not get to know him. He seems afraid, secretive and closed for reasons of being insecure and abashed.

8. EMOTIONAL INTELLIGENCE: This is underestimated in the relationship quotient. Yet, this is what really counts in making and marring of a leader, an organization, a cult, and achieving

a motivated team. It is the ability to work with emotions, both one's own and another's.

9. SENSITIVITY: This may be an inborn trait acquired in early education or a cultivated art. Sensitivity is key to keeping unnecessary hurts and problems at bay. It does not trample on another's toes and stampede another's territory.

10. TRUST: Every leader knows the fundamental importance of trust in building, running and problem solving in organizations. How he manages to build trust, keep trust and work with trust depends on his character not persona. While multiple personalities breed within him and many issues surface, there is one sacred pace which should never be dismantled. It has deep roots, and this is the place of Trust. Trust begets trust. It is, however, seen in some cases trust is betrayed for personal reasons and no explanations rendered. This is because of mood swings, manipulations, and narcissistic tendencies. When calling a spade, a spade is not seen as correction but abrogation it becomes problematic and breeds mistrust.

A leader is not a control-freak boss. He is someone you can approach anytime and have no fear about speaking your mind. He would take the grain and blow the chaff away. Leadership requires self-awareness, a need to understand another's perspective and the ability to give and receive feedback. Communication is the most important skill of a leader. This emanates from within. If he is not a people's person, he had better be one. The job of a leader is more people-oriented than desk-oriented. He has a flock to manage and each of them is an individual. Putting the lid on subjects objectifies people. They do not like it. Those who cannot express their dissent simmer inside till the pressure in the cooker lets off steam. This can have negative results for the entire organization as it stymies progress, projects, and gets the grapevine talking.

Instead, if leaders want to **create a legacy** they need to work towards permanence in relationships. To reach a pinnacle they need to go beyond their tenure. This they can do by providing a platform for future leaders. They are respected for their word, what they represent. They know service before self brings better results than staying in the comfort zone. Leadership is a place to give not receive. Humility is key to leadership. Yet, it is seldom seen, as many live in the bubble of social connexions and become inaccessible to many. Reaching the top is one thing, staying there is another. It needs humility, focus and hard work. An organizational chart helps bring other potential leaders to the fore. Mentoring potential is a way of acknowledging talent. Feedbacks are great.

Creating an inner circle of people who can mirror to the leader his authentic self for the purpose of improving helps. This should not be taken personally as it is in most cases. Thus, learning is lost. Return loyalty the same way. Give them opportunities and blessings. It is a joint journey not a fair-weather friendship. Best way for a leader to grow is to be better tomorrow than what he is today. This way he realizes his potential and helps others realize theirs.

For a leader to be interesting, he must be interested. He must show his interest and actively engage with developing their potential in the projects not just assigning duties. Even a manager can do that. Leadership is more than management. It is not superior or inferior, it is just more. This more entails being effective and being effective entails being there. Presence, Engagement and Responsibility are the three measures with which people judge leaders. There are others of course, but these three dominate. To be credible a leader must be a human being first, change himself before he changes the organization. Everyone has something to teach us. Relationships define who we are and what we become. This is key to people development and must be remembered by the leader. Effectiveness depends upon the climate he creates be it of growth or the grandeur of his persona.

An effective leader is an **alchemist** who changes the negative into positive by being an optimist and shifts the paradigm by effective communication. This brings forth the idea bank, forums, discussions, democratic handling of problems, and more. The atmosphere becomes participative not exclusive.

Good thinkers are always in demand as they are the **kernel of good leadership**. Cultivate them. Associate with them. They open your mind to new perspectives. Don't hush those in your group because of prejudice or personal bias. Listen to the dull and ignorant, they too have their story. Think, Think, and Think things through and develop laser like clarity in yourself. This will let your light shine on others. "Embrace uncertainty." (Leonardo Da Vinci)

CHAPTER EIGHT

CANDOUR

"Caring establishes the relationship. Candour expands it." John C. Maxwell

What is candour and how does it promote leadership relationship?

I have found most positional leaders want sycophants. As long as you are a yes person all is fine. But that limits growth and potential as there is one perspective given importance and that is the leader's. I am not talking about critical thinking here. Candour is often misinterpreted as such. IT is a vast field, simple, spontaneous, coming from the heart – a feedback which must be appreciated and Candour is a two way street.

If your goal is to help the followers, listen to them. Do not block them, restrict them nor tag them. In judging and limiting lie seeds of caste, and its impact is seen today as black lives matter raises its voice, gender discrimination, me groups, swing the tide. All that once was smooth is shaken by erupting volcanoes. Grapevine gains momentum. Then one day: all is blown up in smoke!

It is far better to allow feedback, encourage candour. Give and take it. Kindness and politeness usually go hand in hand.

Wrapping your words and agenda in soft speech because you must get it out there. It is the way you are wired and others expect it of you.

Long term relationships come with trust and candour. It means facing one's demons and angels. Demons first, as the ground must be weeded before it is tilled and prepared for planting.

THIS IS WHAT THE LEADER NEEDS TO DO

Decisions must never be unilateral. They must incorporate another and consider the ripple effect it will have on others. Before deciding, brainstorm your intent, objectives, different perspectives and make room for dissent.

Though everyone has a right to speak, people often have to earn their right to be heard. This they do in many ways. Those who do not, never get heard.

What kind of a leader are you? One who thrusts his opinion and decision or one who actively listens and is it democratic?

Listening extends the platform for the leader and the organization to interact. Out of interaction come ideas, realization of potential, decisions of who goes where. Deputing tasks and appointing people. Right person for the right job, requires active listening, careful consideration of matchmaking theirs with his experience and attributes needed for the job. *How can this be done without candour, feedback, and freedom to express oneself in a conversation directly with the person?*

When you reach a pinnacle, opportunities make a difference and stare at you. Either you grab them and make others into leaders, improve the organization, develop, and use potential or just let it go.

How can all this wisdom be put into action if there is no parleying and active connection. Caring should not supress candour but open up another so he or she can trust to speak the truth, ask questions, help mirror the leader and show another perspective.

Candour does not displace care, but augments it as it is an act of trust and grows out of it. When people restrict others and quantify their speech, ideas, and expressions they are practising systemic racism. It is in the DNA. They grew that way. It was meted out to them, and they are meting it out to others. Choosing leaders and becoming leaders take a lot of inner work.

Being frank and upfront is valued. Developing potential and building momentum are a mix of cognition and feeling. This stirs, encourages and is performative. If you want to use enthusiasm and care in the role, use candour as a means of encouraging others to speak their minds and do not be judging of it. Judgemental attitude is self limiting as it is other limiting.

Practising the rule of 'treating others, as one wants to be treated' always helps. Do not just keep it in mind but exercise it in transactions so there is a paradigm shift and transformative leadership emerges.

CHAPTER NINE

CONCLUSION

In the journey of leadership, what is the takeaway? Why did you accept the role? What did you achieve? How did you and the people you lead grow?

The journey is not spherical like circling the wagons. There is continuum. Unfinished lines are unfinished business. Strong pyramids are pillars supported by vision, values, and community. There are lines and triangles, pyramids, and squares. All these figures stand as differences in approach, execution, and strategies for management and leading. The cautious leader picks the one that he is trained for. The Cautious and Creative leader explores options, perspectives, plans and is ready to adapt. In all cases, the wise leader modulates, accommodates, and aligns himself with the team. He stands behind his people, accepting of differences. He is Creative not Reactive. **Re-active is a reaction from some past pattern played. Response comes from a sense of responsibility**.

Where you posit yourself physically, emotionally, psychologically, and rationally it matters. Relationally speaking proximity matters, so does association. The latter is not only with people but also with ideas.

Interconnectedness is consciousness of the other. It is the apex of a congruent triangle. Influence is developed and reflected by the demeanour of the leader.

Does he influence or is he influenced? Influence lasts longer than power. It is important to ask the question: *"What forces are at play here? Personal bias or humanity?"* Questioning and storytelling are a mode of learning in ancient Hindu texts. Yet, some leaders discourage the practice, so do some teachers in a rush to complete the curriculum.

Leadership is an octopus with its tentacles in all directions but its focus on the mission. The mission is always – people development – task force – developing leaders to be – being team – solving equations – playing roles – being a role model. These traits make a leader succeed. The team is handed to him. What he does with it, how he develops it, is crucial to his stay and success. He who introspects will self correct and be clairvoyant. Enjoy the ride by having fun with each scenario presented. Humour is important. Make light of things and situations, not make a fight of them. Fight or flight tendencies are self defeating exercises. They are evasive and turn to ghosting.

Establish Trust, by trusting first, disclosing first. Communicate this to the team. You are as much the team as the rest of them. Never for a moment think yourself aloof from them, separate from them. This will bring distancing in emotions. Emotional connect is as important as cognitive understanding and appraisal on the job. This awareness is brought through the writing. Leadership is a position of responsibility, of action, thought and effective communication.

Once this recognition and consciousness are taken cognizance of, it becomes easy to navigate the waters and turn mistrust into trust. Once the fundamentals are clear and the mind is open to receive, to appreciate and acknowledge the other, it ceases to be trapped in the isolatory prison of the self. Naturalness and authenticity bring life to the leader. They become his assets. Effortlessness comes in and issues become non-issues.

Life in the fast lane becomes easier. The trod feels the same as the race because he assured his team. The leader has their honesty, their trust and builds upon real foundations. People are dependable if the leader is dependable. Leadership is a character building exercise. It is a relationship that is transformational and not transactional. It is not business where doors are opened and closed at will. More than anything else, it consists of perpetual transitions. Here lessons are learnt. When the leader approaches the post with education and self development in his mind, he builds positive vibes in the team. This scintillates activity, warms hearts and opens minds. A leader who thinks he knows it all and anything goes, is in for disappointments.

Leadership unleashes the potential to **give a voice to the voiceless**, to energize those on the margins, and may never get up from their assigned seats, if they were put down again. These are the people who put leaders in their seats, put up with animosity, arrogance and get ignored. Perhaps this is why Jesus said: "Father forgive them. They are ignorant. They know not what they do?" Aurobindo said: "It is time for collective consciousness to be raised to avoid suffering, liberate the stifled spirit."

CONCLUSION

Trapped in negative silence, handcuffed, and tied to their opinions and decisions, the power drunk and arrogant leader practises hegemony. **Open communication, empathic listening help mitigate differences.**

It is time for a breath of fresh air to liberate the redundancy of worn out measures of judgement; be they 'what is appropriate and what is not'. By whose standards? By whose choice and what is the reason or motive of putting another down, if not a win and lose mentality. This the leader must avoid at every cost. It is a cover up and a cop out. It is counter productive. The catalyst in the leader will shift the paradigm by developing his potential, as well his team in meeting the challenges ahead.

ACKNOWLEDGEMENTS

Many thanks to mentors along the way.

My parents Roshan and Loveleen Varma for trusting me with responsibilities at an incredibly young age. This built my confidence and ability to run the house and tend to my grandparents and younger sister. It helped me organize the day and feed the computer of my mind prioritizing and planning needs versus wants.

Sr. Margaret who built in me the confidence of delivering my first speech to the school upon being elected as the Head Girl of St. Mary's Convent

Dr. Eva Shipstone for her mentoring me and inviting me for Sunday breakfasts while I was the Student Representative of Isabella Thoburn College.

Dr. Bertha May Corfield for putting me on the stage and mentoring theatre devices, usage and more- later honing my skills so I won competitions in directing plays.

Fr. S.J. Wirth for the Leadership Training Course I attended at J.M.C. in Delhi and launched it in Loreto Convents in the country.

Philip Pinto C.F.C. my much valued mentor on this journey for keeping me on track.

Mrs. Anne Pinto for launching my career in Teacher Development programs

Br. Fitzpatrick, my colleague at St. Columba's, New Delhi.

Satish Shrinagesh for his expertise in assisting with Public Speaking engagements for the Corporate world.

Sr. Celine Pinto my trusted friend, music specialist and past Superior at Loreto Convent Calcutta.

H.H. The Dalai Lama for his insights and guiding me on a journey from Delhi to Mumbai.

Mother Teresa who I had the good fortune to meet one to one and spend considerable time with, listening to her leadership role in the community.

Mallika Sarabhai for providing avenues like the BBC and BCL to showcase my poetry, writing and theatre as a learning and healing tool.

Brian Beal for getting me back to writing.

My daughter Diya for teaching me patience.

My husband Anil and son Manik for the role they played in life and learning.

The Publisher for bringing it to the public.

Last but not the least to the Eternal spirit that energizes and moves the finger to write.

BIBLIOGRAPHY

Cristopher Saunders, *Leadership*, Oxford University Press, 2020

Ken Roe, *Leadership Practice and Perspective*, Oxford University Press, 2017

Julian Barling, *The Science of Leadership*, Oxford University Press, 2014

Jo Owen, *Myths of Leadership*, Oxford University Press, 2017

Scott Snook, Nitin Noria, Rakesh Khurana, *The Handbook for Teaching Leadership*, Oxford University Press, 2012

Barbara Kellerman, *Bad Leadership*, Harvard University Review

John P. Kotter, *Leading Change*, Harvard University Review Press, 2012

Daniel Goleman, *What Makes A Leader*, Harvard University Review Press, 2017

Daniel Goleman, *Working with Emotional Intelligence*, Harvard University Review Press

Daniel Goleman, *Destructive Emotions: A Scientific Dialogue with the Dalai Lama*, Harvard University Review Press, 2000

John C. Maxwell, *How Successful People Lead*, Center Street, New York, 2013

Michael J. Gelb, *How to Think like Leonardo da Vinci*, Bantam Dell/Random House, 1998

BY THE SAME AUTHOR

Significance of Signs (2021) is an experiential journey into love and fear – explored through the lens of signs. This book reflects on synchronicities, coincidences, and more, to help us understand the nature of things, relationships, events and ourselves. ISBN 978-1638293644

Commodifying Seniors (2021) is an East-West perspective on seniors that emphasises different lenses and different perceptions of seniors and care-givers in a conversational and experiential format. Its intention is to build awareness that 'senior' does not mean senile and that there is no 'mental menopause'. ISBN 978-1649796295

Cultural Awakenings: Insightful Writings (2020) Written in an experiential, story-telling manner, this is a book of insightful reading on human issues that we all face. Recommended reading for all those who wish to go beyond the nitty gritty of superficial living, and apply learning to life, thus making life meaningful. ISBN 978-1-912662-22-7 (Hansib)

Cultural Conundrums: Poems on Inter-Connectedness (2015)
This book is about seeing the world with different lenses so that 'different' is not 'alien'. The norms of the East and West sometimes bring about a clash of perceptions and create cultural conundrums. Much is lost in interpretation, much is misunderstood and walls emerge where a bridge could easily connect. ISBN 978-1-910553-19-0 (Hansib)

Signature Cultures: Poems that Awaken Consciousness (2013)
These poems raise the questions that have remained unanswered for ages. The questions are important as behind/beside each question there could be a mysterious door to the unknown. Just like a painting shows not just a scene, but also the emotions the painter, these poems give us a glimpse into the anguish and questioning of a soul that feels life crowding in and equally feels the need to be true to herself. ISBN 978-1-906190-61-3 (Hansib)